Praise

Where the Saints Came From

Where the Saints Came From is a fascinating kaleidoscope of places, stories and insights from across Wales and spanning the centuries. Anne offers something for the casual reader as well as for travellers and pilgrims: anecdotes and nuggets of historical colour which draw the reader in and make you want to visit in person, stop and drink in the significance of each place.

Clive Orchard, Warden and Team Leader
Ffald-y-Brenin Trust

In this book Anne shows herself to be both a pilgrim and also a guide: firstly she is the curious, purposeful traveller, a stranger through territory that takes her away from the familiar of home; yet she is very much at home with the discoveries and knowledge she shares about the journey and the destinations of her travel. This fascinating travelogue is a cornucopia of history, spirituality and a guide which captures something of the richness of Welsh Christian culture and tradition through two millennia. Through her detail and embracing chapters, Anne inspires and invites the reader to set off for themselves to discover the worlds of faith, biography, architecture and legend which exist alongside the busy highways as well as the serene byways of this island's rich rural and urban landscape. This is a work that joins the rich body of journeys through Wales by, among others, Giraldus Cambrensis, Samuel Johnson and Mrs Thrale, and George Borrow. A delight to read at the fireside, a handy manual to take on the road.

The Right Reverend Peter M. Brignall
Bishop of Wrexham

To Norma Thomas, with many thanks

Where the Saints Came From

ON PILGRIMAGE IN
WALES AND BEYOND

ANNE HAYWARD

Cover design: Y Lolfa
Cover photographs: Anne Hayward
Top, L–R: St Maughold, Ramsey, Isle of Man; St Samson, Caldey;
Churchyard cross, Tremeirchion. Bottom,
L–R: Stained-glass window, Blaenau Ffestiniog;
Medieval cross, Lonan Old Church.

ISBN: 978 1 80099 486 7

Published and printed in Wales
on paper from well-maintained forests by
Y Lolfa Cyf., Talybont, Ceredigion SY24 5HE
website www.ylolfa.com
e-mail ylolfa@ylolfa.com
tel 01970 832 304

Contents

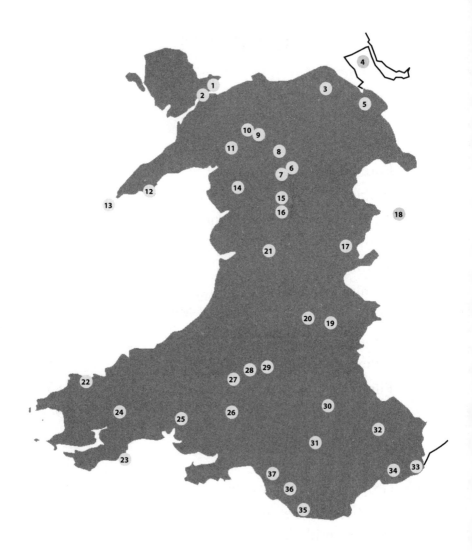

1   Church of Our Lady Queen of Martyrs, Beaumaris
2   St Tysilio's Church, Menai Bridge
3   The churchyard cross, Tremeirchion
4   Holy Cross Church, Woodchurch
5   The Gladstone Library, Hawarden
6   Our Lady of Fatima Catholic Church, Bala
7   Mary Jones Pilgrim Centre, Llanycil

Foreword

WALES IS KNOWN across the earth as being a nation which has encountered God through incredible revivals, for thousands of people coming to know the Lord Jesus in amazing moves of God. Church and chapel buildings punctuate our streets; our huge catalogue of hymns still resonate around our sport stadia; and we're a nation who have sent scores of missionaries across the globe to proclaim the Good News of Jesus Christ, changing the eternal direction of not only souls but nations. What a glorious heritage we possess.

Pilgrimage lies deep in the heart of the Christian faith. Take for example the account of Abraham in the book of Genesis leaving his home in search of a land God had promised to show him; or the account of the exodus from Egypt where the Israelites spent forty years wandering in the desert before being led into the Promised Land by Joshua. Psalm 84 describes pilgrims walking through the dry and sorrowful valley of Baka, and making it into a place of springs, each one going from strength to strength until they appear before God in Zion. Later, in the New Testament we read of crowds descending upon the city of Jerusalem three times a year to worship the Lord and be taught from scripture.

Pilgrimages are often undertaken with a sense of expectation of a deepening connection with God, where the pilgrim allows themselves space to experience those thin places where the gap between heaven and earth becomes tiny or even nonexistent. Frequently there is a renewed sense of peace, purpose, and inevitably transformation as each step readies the pilgrim for the destination. For centuries, these were seen as some of life's greatest adventures, a journey along a road that might ultimately lead to an encounter with God.

What if a pilgrimage was less about visiting a shrine or sacred place, but instead a journey towards a personal relationship with God? Your personal pilgrimage matters. In the words of Pastor Rick Warren, 'At most, you will live a hundred years on earth, but you will spend forever in eternity.' My prayer as you read this book is that we will all be able to echo the words of the famous Welsh hymnwriter, William Williams, who wrote:

> Guide me, O thou great Redeemer,
> Pilgrim through this barren land;
> I am weak, but thou art mighty;
> Hold me with thy powerful hand:
> When I tread the verge of Jordan,
> Bid my anxious fears subside;
> Death of death, and hell's destruction,
> Land me safe on Canaan's side.

Siân Wyn Rees
Head of Bible Society, Wales

Preface

FOR SOME TIME now I have been fortunate, and also very privileged, in being able to spend several months each year walking on pilgrimage in Britain and beyond. Setting out soon after Easter from my home in the Bannau Brycheiniog area of mid Wales, I make my way to a significant Christian site and then walk back again by a different route.

I can describe these pilgrimages as not only a delight and a joy but also as a great source of learning and discovery, for as I walk, not only do I come across a very considerable variety of different churches and other places relevant to the rich religious history of the British Isles, but I'm also able to visit many secluded or little-known gems that can be found tucked away on rolling hillsides or in quiet streets in urban areas.

It's sometimes said of pilgrimage that what matters is the journey rather than the destination. I would hope that what I have selected to include in this book lends support to that view – with a range that is deliberately eclectic and with a considerable proportion being in outdoor locations, the topics covered vary widely. In all, over forty sites are discussed, with the material being arranged in roughly chronological order to broadly follow the development of the Christian faith in Wales from the later Roman period up to the present day.

But, in the weeks and months that I spend in all sorts of interesting places, I also often find myself chatting with people whom I encounter along the way. One of those conversations, enjoyed when I was in Brittany (*Llydaw*), inspired the title of this book. Discussing my plans to walk on the traditional pilgrimage route known as the Tro-Breiz[1] with a lady I met in the Morlaix (*Montroulez*) area, I explained that I lived in Wales and had walked from there. At that point she continued my sentence, adding: 'where the saints came from'.

On her part, this person's comment stemmed from the continuing close ties between Brittany and Wales and, in particular, the Breton tradition of the Welsh origins of their early medieval founder saints. However, her words also struck me as being prescient of the remarkable story of religious faith in Wales, not only in the Age of the Saints to which the *saints fondateurs* belong, but also in later times and into our own day. Of course I am biased, but I am convinced that nowhere else has packed quite so much interest into so small a nation.

Many people much more learned than me have also written about the history of the Welsh Church, in its broadest sense, and to these scholars I am deeply indebted. Also, more general writers and those whose expertise extends into many other spheres have been a great resource and inspiration; but I still wanted to share something of my own findings and research, these being rooted in my long-distance walking which has now covered many thousands of miles.

My two previous books were both based on specific treks: *A Pilgrimage Around Wales* was structured around recollections of encounters I had as I made my way the very first time, while my second book, *A Celtic Pilgrimage*, resulted from my travels to Brittany the following year.

But I found that in each succeeding adventure I acquired what seemed to be yet more promising material, much of which I came across in Wales or that had some relevance to my adopted home. In addition, I found that I still had useful observations made on those first two pilgrimages that I had not yet been able to include. Above all, I found myself wanting to write a volume that was more greatly orientated towards history rather than the more general topics and the spirituality of pilgrimage as had been the case with my previous writing. I would have to stress, though, that it is only in the most tentative of tones that I can describe myself as a historian.

In selecting material for *Where the Saints Came From*, all the places featured have been arrived at by me on foot on what have now become annual walks, and it is my intention that those who kindly read this book will be aware that what I write about has arisen through this very personal means. The great majority of sites I discuss are, of course, in Wales itself, but just a few have been selected from England and further afield, these being places that have a clear connection with Wales, or where particular sites are useful in encouraging a greater understanding of the story of the Welsh Christian experience, not least on my own part.

But now, I could, perhaps, be found guilty of boasting!

As already mentioned, I initially made two long-distance walks, these both being very formative times. However, since then I have made my way across Wales to Glendalough in Ireland, a place of pilgrimage dating back to the sixth century, and also to the Isle of Man, as well as to places such as Lichfield, Walsingham and St Albans in England.

In addition, in order to extend what I have done and to explore further in areas I have passed through only briefly, I also undertake an extra pilgrimage later in the year. So far, this has allowed me to walk north as far as the island of Iona (*Ì Chaluim Chille*), on the west coast of Scotland, and also to make my way, much closer to home, across south Wales and the post-industrial Valleys for which the area is renowned.

Bearing everything else in mind, I have tried to provide a reasonable spread across Wales of the places I have selected for discussion in this book. However, with my custom being to walk from home and back again (my pilgrimages are, in effect, very long circular walks), it requires perhaps only a modest awareness of Welsh geography to discern that some areas feature rather more fully than others. For this I offer my apologies and my determination that I will set out across the Cambrian Mountains (*Mynyddoedd Cambria/Elenydd*) and the inland areas of Ceredigion as soon as I can.

I would also have to add that I am very much aware that some important themes are only touched upon rather briefly, if at all (an example would be the great tradition of hymn composition and singing), but I hope that topics as varied as Roman roads in Wales, the metallurgy of early medieval bell-founding, the development of Quaker graveyards, and the re-invention of an early saint in contemporary literature will be some compensation.

Meanwhile, as regards the practicalities of walking, I always follow public rights of way and find that National Trails and Recreational Paths as indicated on Ordnance Survey maps are particularly useful. Within Wales, these include the Wales Coast Path (*Llwybr Arfordir Cymru*), the Offa's Dyke Path (*Llwybr Clawdd Offa*), the Wye Valley Walk (*Llwybr Dyffryn Gwy*) and the North Wales Pilgrim's Way (*Taith Pererin Gogledd Cymru*).

As to language, I have given place-names, and other significant features, as they are used by English speakers. In many cases, the names of towns, villages and so on are the same for everyone. But, in cases where the Welsh name is different to that used in English, I have put this following the English name but after the first mention only. I have done the same, but making use of the relevant Celtic language, as regards places in Cornwall, the Isle of Man, Ireland and Scotland, while both French and Breton names are given as appropriate in Brittany. As to the rather complex issue of the different versions of their names given to some of the early saints, I have tried to be consistent in using the form as it occurs in the place that is the main focus.

I have also tried to ensure that all historical terms, with which some readers may not be familiar, are explained in context, although I think it is always useful to point out that the centuries between the end of the Roman occupation and the arrival of the Normans in Wales constitute the early medieval period. As the same era in England is often described as Anglo-

Saxon, I have found that some confusion can occur among those who are more used to dealing with English history. Fundamental to all this, of course, is an understanding that Wales never became an Anglo-Saxon kingdom.

In relation to this, I have also used the word 'Celtic' to describe what is seen as culturally specific to Wales in the early medieval period (and, in addition, to the wider area of the western seaboard of Britain as well as other regions so far as they remained outside the Anglo-Saxon kingdoms). Rooted in our understanding of the Iron Age and pre-Roman life in the British Isles, this word is also used to discuss the continuing shared heritage of what are sometimes called the Celtic nations. I appreciate that this use is problematic for some but, to me, it seems a convenient term. Moreover, the use of 'British' as an alternative, as was often the case with historians and antiquarians of earlier generations, can lead to just another set of complications for today's readers even though, strictly speaking, it is more accurate.

Meanwhile, this might be an appropriate place to mention that, as any discussion of the Christian faith in Wales involves introducing some of the early saints to whom a considerable proportion of churches in Wales are dedicated, these people are what are sometimes referred to as pre-congregational saints. This is because the Roman Catholic Church, which is usually taken as the measure of these things, did not have a process of canonisation until the twelfth century. In this, Wales is the same as the rest of the British Isles and also further afield.

Also, for better or for worse, as these documents have a reputation for a great deal of fanciful detail, much of what we can know of the early saints is from their 'Lives', or *Vitae*, written in Latin and often several centuries after the lifetime of the person in question. In my writing, I also generally use this Latin term when discussing examples of these texts. Particular discussion of the value, or otherwise, of *Vitae* is found in chapters 2 and 10 in relation to St Tugdual and St Samson respectively.

All dates, unless otherwise stated, are CE.

Finally, although I am well aware of the joys of discovery when sitting comfortably in an armchair, I would of course hope that this modest volume encourages its readers to go out and explore for themselves wherever possible This would not only be the places and artefacts I have described but, more importantly, those that haven't made their way into this book. These could include: a former church (now a private house) with a magnificent Byzantine-style ceiling; the welcoming south Wales chapel which houses the grave of the couple who, until recently, were the longest married in Britain; the delicate stone sculpture which might, just, be a Romano-British image of one of the early saints; the church with a visitors' book in which can be seen the signatures of Italian prisoners taken to the church during the Second World War, and so on.

All these, and far more besides, are waiting for their next visitor.

Anne Hayward
Pilgrim Street Contemporary Pilgrimage
March 2024

CHAPTER 1

A town centre car park and the beginnings of the Christian faith in Wales

I HAVE LONG been fascinated with the historical context in which the New Testament stories take place, that is, the Roman Empire, the superpower of the day. Whether it's St Paul's eventful final journey to Rome,[1] where it is assumed that he met his death by execution during the reign of Nero (reigned 54–68) or the familiar words of St Luke's gospel: 'there went out a decree from Caesar Augustus that all the world should be taxed'[2] with which the narrative of Jesus' birth begins, we can't get away from the all-powerful nature of imperial rule. However, the Roman Empire also provided the context by which the Christian faith first reached our corner of Europe, with archaeology providing evidence, albeit limited, of the arrival of the new religion in Wales by the late third century.

Moreover, as a long-distance walker and pilgrim, I'm often reminded of the occupation of much of Britain as I pass everything from the sites of ports and wharves, to signalling stations, bath houses and amphitheatres, all dating back to this very formative period of our history. With so much still to see, the Romans seem to be almost everywhere. We even continue to walk (or now drive) along the course of their roads, something our forebears have also been doing for over fifteen hundred years!

Consequently, I have chosen five quite different places in

mid and north Wales to feature in this chapter, not least to draw attention away from the more Romanised areas of the south-east of the country.[3]

Two of my choices, the amphitheatre at Carmarthen (*Caerfyrddin*) and the road known as Sarn Helen, have no immediately obvious religious connection, but perhaps symbolise something of the wider legacy of Roman rule in Wales. But, above all, perhaps each of the places I focus on draws attention to how difficult, if not impossible, it is to disentangle the features of the Roman period from what follows in the succeeding few centuries and how little we actually know of this era.

Castle Car Park, Llandovery

OS: SN 768 344

A few phrases on the tourist information board in a car park in Llandovery (*Llanymddyfri*) perhaps serve as an unlikely introduction to the question of how Christianity arrived in Wales and what might have been the extent of the new religion in what was then the western section of the Roman province of *Britannia*.

In the centre of this Carmarthenshire (*Sir Gaerfyrddin*) town and close to the remains of the Norman castle, it is explained that the first known settlement in the area was the *vicus* that grew up around the fort of *Alabum*,[4] just to the north of contemporary Llandovery. However, this simple early settlement serving the needs of the occupying power 'did not survive the fall of the Roman Empire ... but it is thought that Christianity was introduced during the Roman period and certainly remained'.[5]

Hence, Llandovery, with one of its medieval parish churches built within the site of the fort, is perhaps a good place to start discussing the many and varied factors relating to the Christian faith in its earliest days in Wales. Walking through the town as

I made my way on pilgrimage from Lichfield in the midlands of England to Llandeilo in west Wales, I was intrigued by what I read on the issue of the religion's arrival during the Roman occupation and its possible continuation after the withdrawal of the imperial forces.

The information board is rightly reticent about what can be known about the local area, but one question we don't need to ask is whether Christianity made some inroads into Wales in general during the Roman period. This is most definitely the case, notably because artefacts that are clearly associated with the new faith have been found among Roman remains. As with similar finds in England, items such as the Caerwent bowl with its *chi-rho* inscription[6] give us tentative evidence for some degree of Christian belief in what would have been quite a far-flung area, close to the edge of the Empire.

And while this simple artefact may provide something tangible which can be seen and examined, Wales is also the setting of the notable tradition of the Christian martyrs Julius and Aaron meeting their deaths in the Roman legionary fortress of *Isca Augustus*, now Caerleon (*Caerllion*) and only a few miles from Caerwent, probably in around 300. Described by the sixth-century churchman Gildas, and later attested to by Bede (673–735) in his *Ecclesiastical History of the English People*, the evidence for Julius and Aaron dying for their faith is further supported by evidence of at least one church dedicated to each of them in the early medieval period in the Caerleon area and a considerable proliferation by the time of the Normans. And although there is some suggestion that the two martyrs may have met their deaths at Chester (*Caer*) and not in Caerleon, it is their names that provide the greatest clue as to how the Christian faith may have reached these shores, in that neither name is one indigenous to Britain. This is a timely reminder that the Roman forces in *Britannia* contained individuals from across an Empire where the new faith was expanding rapidly.

Of course, Wales would have been no different to other areas where the easy mobility brought about by the Empire's need for good communications brought with it those who identified as Christians. Julius and Aaron are generally thought of as Roman soldiers (and as such are likely to have been beheaded), but even if they were civilians involved in the *vicus* alongside the fortress at Caerleon, their names testify to the most likely means by which the Roman faith reached Britain, that is as a consequence of the movement of personnel and the ideas and beliefs that they brought with them.

But did the Christian faith reach the Llandovery area in the Roman period as the information board suggests might have been the case? Could forts at a distance from the more Romanised areas of the south-east of Wales have had their own equivalents of Julius and Aaron in people who had arrived from other provinces of the Empire?

Perhaps the most helpful way to look at this question is to appreciate that the evidence for Christianity in England as well as in Wales at this time is primarily associated with Roman military and civilian settlements, and not with the wider countryside. And although the fort at *Alabum* is thought to have been discontinued in the mid second century, and the *vicus* may well not have survived, it is quite plausible that tiny numbers of followers of the new religion may have found their way here, this seeming particularly likely after the legalisation of Christianity within the Roman Empire in 313 and its adoption as the official faith ten years later.

It has been estimated that there may have been as many as five million people who identified as Christians within the Empire as a whole by this time. And, although the spread of the new faith is thought to have been uneven, it seems reasonable to think that perhaps just a very few of that number would be found in this area of mid Wales, placed as it was at the junction of two major roads, with their good connections onwards to the west and north, and also its proximity to the valuable gold mines at nearby Dolaucothi. With these being managed and worked by specialist contractors, the Llandovery area would have drawn in civilian as well as military personnel, adding to the likelihood that adherents of the new faith may have been among them.[7]

The Roman Amphitheatre at Carmarthen

OS: SN 419 206

The remains of the amphitheatre at Carmarthen can be seen from the A484 about a quarter of a mile from the town centre, with grassy banks and some sections of restored Roman stonework indicating the site of the most westerly known amphitheatre in Britain. An information board shows a reconstruction of how it would have looked in its heyday, drawing attention to how this structure was situated outside the walls of Roman Carmarthen alongside the road that led to the east gate of what was then *Moridunum*.

The building of what are now busy dual-carriageways, which only the northern side of the town has avoided, has had the effect of making the amphitheatre seem tucked away in a side street, but the A484 follows the course of what would have been one of the arterial roads in Roman Wales. With a capacity to hold over four thousand people on tiered, wooden seating erected on a stone base, it would have been a very impressive sight in its time. Being used for military and civic parades and perhaps occasional gladiatorial contests, it is one of only seven of these structures known to have been built in Britain.

The information at the site explains how the local Borough Surveyor, George Ovens, suspecting that an oval hollow might be the site of an amphitheatre and being able to protect it from development, led to its excavation in the 1960s. With other Roman buildings including shops, a bath house and a temple having been discovered earlier in the twentieth century, a more complete picture of Roman Carmarthen then emerged.

However, the amphitheatre is the only structure of which remains have been preserved above ground.[8]

Ancient *Moridunum*, still shadowed in the town plan of the Carmarthen we see today, was built in about 75 as the imperial forces attempted to push north and west from the easier territory in the Vale of Glamorgan (*Bro Morgannwg*). With other forts accessible from the sea, in Cardiff (*Caerdydd*), Neath (*Castell-nedd*) and Loughor (*Casllwchwr*), Carmarthen may have been one of a line of fortifications supplied by a fleet based on the coast of south Wales as well as being a junction for roads to the north and also further to the west. But what of the role of *Moridunum* and its amphitheatre in the story of where the saints came from?

To consider this issue, it has to be remembered that in the second century the Romans relinquished their direct rule in Carmarthen and the surrounding area and handed it over to the local tribe, the *Demetae*, who held it as a *civitas* on their overlord's behalf. With Caerwent being the only other such town in Wales, the handing over to the *Demetae* represented a considerable victory for Romanisation in this area. The native people had become like the Romans themselves, and were no longer seen as a threat but as an integral part of the Empire.

With a planned system of streets and roads, public buildings and bath houses, *Moridunum* would have taken its place as a *civitas* not only with Caerwent but also similar settlements not far away in Wroxeter and Cirencester, as well as those further afield, such as in what are now Leicester and Winchester. And although it was only ever small by the standards of Roman towns, Carmarthen's status as a *civitas* surely says a lot for second-century west Wales.

There's also just a possibility that the early 'bishop house' of Llan Teulydawc,[9] believed to have been on the site of St Peter's Church, may have had its origins in Roman Carmarthen. As our understanding grows of *civitates* (the plural form) as the centres of early bishoprics in southern and central Britain, it may be that *Moridunum* was one of these and that this evolved into Llan Teulydawc. In addition, a sideways step then leads to consideration that the survival of post-Roman bishoprics in the midlands of England (in areas that were yet to be subsumed into the pagan Anglo-Saxon kingdoms being established from the south and east) could have been a further factor in the Christianisation of Wales.[10]

The Penmachno stones

OS: SH 790 506

Penmachno was a great find for me as a pilgrim for all sorts of reasons. St Tudclud's remains the only church I have ever visited which had a coffee and hot drinks machine available for visitors to use!

On a more serious note, though, the building was closed for public worship for several years but was later re-opened. When I visited it had been in its current re-ordered state, with provision for use as a community hub as well as a space set aside for religious services, for about ten years.

However, it was the church's collection of ancient stones, four of them with Latin inscriptions, that particularly interested me that day. Dating from perhaps the late fifth to the sixth centuries, they provide us with fascinating glimpses into life in Wales in the immediate post-Roman period.[11]

All sorts of things can be observed about the Penmachno stones which with our modern eyes and ways of thinking can easily be overlooked. Firstly, that they exist at all, for it was only in Roman times in Britain that stones were first worked and inscribed with text for the purpose of remembering or commemorating the dead, a tradition that then continued. In addition, such stones also demonstrate the new literacy that came with Roman culture, that is, written Latin in what had been a pre-literate society speaking the Brittonic language of Iron Age Britain.

But the particularly interesting nature of what can be seen in this village church relates to the dating of its collection to the century or so following the end of Roman rule in Wales, making them an extraordinary indicator of what some aspects of life might have been like at a time we know very little about. Above all, they make us think about how far Roman culture and institutions remained an influence after the formal ending of the Empire.[12]

In addition, the inscriptions on the stones have varying degrees of complexity in the language used as well as considerable variation in how well the legibility has been preserved as regards our experience of them today. However, all are believed to be Christian in origin in that the phrases that are used are those that evolved across the Roman Empire in association with the new faith.

One of the examples, the *Carausius* stone, also includes the *chi-rho* symbol already noted as regards the Caerwent bowl. Moreover, as Christian monuments, they provide good evidence that the religion which had made its way to Britain in the Roman period survived the withdrawal of the imperial forces, and had become to some extent part of the indigenous culture in this upland region.

The stones also give us some tempting clues as to whether Roman systems of government lingered on in this area, even after the original reason for their existence had gone. One stone refers to the deceased as a 'citizen' and cousin of a 'magistrate', although just what these very Roman terms would have meant in post-Imperial Wales is unclear.

The place of north Wales in the wider post-Roman world is another aspect of the Penmachno inscriptions, in that one of them uses the imperial system of using consulships as a means of dating, even though this was becoming obsolete in western Europe at the time. This has led to the suggestion that this part of Wales had connections with specific areas on the Continent where the same system was still in use. However, there is also the possibility that the consul in question was the then eastern emperor in Constantinople, with the inference that some people in Wales at this time saw themselves as part of the Empire that still persisted in the east.

However, perhaps most importantly, the Latin of the Penmachno stones also gives us a big hint about how language would continue to develop in the post-Roman world. Not only was Latin understood and written in north Wales[13] but that same language would go on to become the medieval and church Latin which was such a unifying force even after the Empire to which it had uniquely belonged had disintegrated in Western Europe.

It is certainly challenging to think that the mountains of Eryri had their place in this emerging, Christian Europe, with its advantage of mutually-intelligible language in worship, scholarship and communications with other regions. Meanwhile, moving on a thousand years or so, Penmachno was also the birthplace of Bishop William Morgan (1545–1604), the noted translator of the Bible into Welsh. His family home at Tŷ Mawr Wybrnant is owned by the National Trust.

The Melus Medicus stone

OS: 296 289

The *Melus Medicus* stone in the churchyard of St Cian's church at Llangian near Abersoch provides another glimpse into the post-Roman world in Wales. Broadly contemporary with the Penmachno stones, its Latin wording, MELI MEDICI FILI MARTINI IACET (a lower case was yet to develop), is unique in Britain in being the only early inscription to mention the profession, with this being clearly civilian and not either ecclesiastical or military, of the person commemorated: Melus the doctor.

The pillar-type stone is thought to be a grave marker and, although we can't be sure that it's in its original position, it could be evidence for St Cian's possibly being an early religious site, with archaeological excavations in the churchyard having resulted in evidence for human activity here in about 550. With the inclusion of IACET *he lies (here)*, the *Melus Medicus* stone is believed to be a specifically Christian memorial, like those at Penmachno.[14]

However, the Latin on the stone may also be indicative of settlement from Ireland in this area of north Wales. This is because the text is written vertically, this being a characteristic of early Irish Ogham[15] inscriptions, as is the additional phrase denoting *Melus* as the son of *Martinus*, this formulaic wording denoting kinship being commonplace in Irish inscriptions but almost unknown in those of Roman origin. The Llangian stone thus hints at the wider issue of cross-cultural influence from across the Irish Sea at this time.

Medicus is also important from a Welsh-language perspective in that it's the root of *meddyg*, the word for 'doctor' in modern Welsh[16] and one of several hundred Latin words that made their way into Brittonic as then spoken in Wales.

As I walked around Wales on pilgrimage, I had lots of happy memories of this area from holidays there as a child, including visiting Llangian. However, one of my recollections is of my father buying a booklet with the title *Welsh in a Week* from a shop in Abersoch; even as a nine or ten year old, I remember thinking that this was quite an ambitious undertaking.

As regards the huge growth of tourism on this part of the Llŷn peninsula (*Pen Llŷn*), it's interesting to note that although Abersoch is now by far the biggest village, the local Community Council takes its name from the much more ancient settlement at Llanengan. The extremely high property prices remain a cause for debate, as does the low level of Welsh speaking in an area where many were born outside out of Wales. Not everyone has shared my father's enthusiasm.

Sarn Helen

OS: SH 722 296

On my pilgrimages I meet all sorts of people along the way and very much enjoy chatting, often in response to kind enquiries as to what I'm doing. I suppose the sight of a solitary woman carrying considerable-sized backpack is quite likely to elicit curiosity and I often get into conversations as I walk. By their very nature, these chats are unlikely to be resumed as both parties need to carry on with their journey. However, on this occasion I met the same couple in their impressive vehicle three times over the course of an hour or two; they were exploring a track high on a hillside in north-west Wales, this being classified by the Ordnance Survey as 'Other route with public access'.[17] Each time we met we all stopped, having an interesting discourse albeit in three sections.

I have to admit that, at first, I was a little surprised to meet this couple in their sturdy Land Rover. As a pedestrian, I often imagine that the tracks and paths I find so helpful and convenient are intended only for non-motorised transport. But coming across these people was a reminder that I was on a Roman road originally intended not only for the legions and the efficient imperial postal service, but also the trade and communications that were so important within the Roman Empire. How fitting that both 'off-roading' enthusiasts and long-distance walkers should be using such a route almost two thousand years later.

The Roman road that we all found ourselves on that day was a section of what is often referred to as Sarn Helen,[18] the north-south artery in west Wales which at this point runs almost parallel to the modern A470 between Dolgellau and Trawsfynydd. Unlike the main road below, the older road follows a course high on the hillside with spectacular views over to the Rhinog mountains (*Rhinogydd*) to the west, and on my right as I walked south that day.

However, this beautiful route is by no means the only

27

section of Roman road in Wales that I have made use of on my pilgrimages. Closer to home, I have also walked along the ancient track that skirts just to the north of the Bannau Brycheiniog between Trecastle (*Trecastell*) and Llandovery. This also takes an upland course, while the busy A40 which has succeeded it keeps to the valley below. As with the section of Sarn Helen between Dolgellau and Trawsfynydd, here too features such as the *agger* and the *vallum* can be seen as reminders of the origins of these routes as Roman roads.[19]

But if such features are in many places evident even today, and the road itself in both these cases continues in its usefulness both for 'off-road' vehicles and those of us on foot, it also has to be asked how much Roman roads were made use of in the post-imperial period in Wales? With such good means of communication already in existence, could these routes have been utilised by the early saints on their travels?

On this point, the Roman roads perhaps speak for themselves, notably the ease with which some of their courses can still be followed in the early twenty-first century, as clearly demonstrated in the examples above. Moreover, my observations as a walker follow in the much more distinguished footsteps of pioneers in this field, notably the antiquarian and engineer Thomas Codrington (1829–1918), whose surveys in the late nineteenth century included not only his own detailed notes but also comparisons with what had been seen by others as far back as the sixteenth century.[20] Going back another thousand years or so, it hardly seems unreasonable to assume that the Roman roads of Wales were in good and usable condition and a factor in the spread of the Christian faith.

A particular proponent of this view was the geographer, E.G. Bowen (1900–1983), the author of *Settlements of the Celtic Saints in Wales*. Keen to analyse the siting of churches in relation to features in the landscape, both natural and man-made, Bowen put forward the view that Roman roads were a specific determining factor in the distribution of churches dedicated to St Padarn. This was because he observed that dedications to other early saints were often in clusters, whereas Padarn's churches followed a roughly linear arrangement on a north-south axis. With four of these in west Wales and not far from Sarn Helen,[21] and another three over the eastern side of the Cambrian Mountains and also close to a Roman road,[22] it is hard not to come to the conclusion that such means of communication was significant, whether followed personally by Padarn or by later followers or disciples.

Meanwhile, Bowen's theories have since been very much challenged and the distribution of dedications to Celtic saints is now seen as the result of a wide range of factors. However, his fascinating book, with its determined emphasis on historical geography, remains essential reading on many counts.

CHAPTER 2

Setting Sail

THIS CHAPTER IS concerned with the importance of the sea, and the associated phenomenon of migration, in the inter-connected histories not only of Wales and Brittany but also the most westerly counties of England, that is Somerset, Devon and Cornwall. This was an aspect of Welsh history that I had only very limited awareness of before I set out on pilgrimage for the first time. However, meeting a Belgian couple who were doing a campervan tour of the Celtic nations had encouraged me to learn more and was, perhaps, the deciding factor in my choice to go to Brittany the following year.[1]

In retrospect it also now seems particularly apt that I met these intrepid travellers near the town of Corwen in Denbighshire (*Sir Ddinbych*), where the parish church is dedicated to saints Mael and Sulien, who may have come to Wales from that area of what is now western France.

However, the travels of these men, and others like them at a time which is sometimes rather poetically referred to as the Age of the Saints, would have taken place in the context of the wider-scale movements of peoples which were a key factor not only in the decline of the western Empire, especially from the fourth century – and its eventual fall in the 470s, but also in the post-Roman period; specifically, Wales would have seen people arriving from the north of Britain and from Ireland, as already mentioned in relation to the *Melus Medicus* stone. Also, Mael and Sulien are a reminder that, as regards the travels of the early saints, who were often drawn from the very mobile aristocracy of the time, migration and settlement seem to have moved in both directions.

But now, with boats carrying people, together with their ideas, beliefs, language and yet more, we start on the shore of the Bristol Channel (*Môr Hafren*) near the town of Llantwit Major (*Llanilltud Fawr*), then continue to the picturesque port of Fowey (*Fowydh*) on the south coast of Cornwall before completing our voyage at the parish church in the village of Langoat (*Langoad*) in Brittany. There, a saint commemorated in the names of islands off the coast of north Wales is depicted with his mother on a splendid tomb, just a few kilometres from the cathedral which bears his name.

The Afon Col-huw near Llantwit Major

OS: SS 957 674

Llantwit Major is a small town close to where the little Afon (river) Col-huw meets the sea. There, where surfers gather and people walk through on the Wales Coast Path, an information board declares that this was 'once one of the most important towns in the world'. This may be something of an overstatement but the confident tone is encouraging as I would have to say that, in my experience, there seems to be a far greater awareness in Brittany of the historical significance of Llantwit Major than there is in Wales.[2]

However, the coastline at this point is now quite different from how it would have looked when boats would land and travellers disembark here in the heyday of Llantwit Major as a very considerable religious centre in the early medieval period. For here, at what can seem to be a rather unassuming suburban area, was situated what today we might call a seminary, with its former students appearing to have been among the key figures in the Christianisation not only of Brittany and of the south-west of England, but also within what is now Wales.

Moreover, the history and changing nature of the coastline

of this part of south Wales has become even more interesting, in that there is now evidence that, until about the sixteenth century, there was a late-medieval harbour approximately 200 metres seaward from the present shoreline. Due to the softness of the local rock, this section of the coast has eroded away since that time but some timbers and masonry have remained in place, coming to the notice of geomorphologists in the late twentieth century. Together with some contemporary documentary evidence, the existence of a lost port near Llantwit Major was proposed in 1991.[3]

The case for such a long-gone feature in this area of the Glamorgan (*Morgannwg*) coast seems not only considerable but would also have implications for Llantwit Major being accessed from the sea in the more distant past, and how it might have functioned as something like a channel port in the Age of the Saints.

The current appearance of the river mouth is also deceptive as to how it might have looked many years ago. With the river now having to flow through a shingle bank, the studies carried out on the existence of the lost port have confirmed that this is relatively modern. It's also perhaps pertinent to point out that there are ongoing debates as to whether this area of the coast has been affected by dredging, since the 1920s, in the Bristol Channel and whether this has led to the loss of sand on the shoreline at Llantwit Major and further to the west towards Porthcawl.[4]

Of course, there is no evidence that in the Age of the Saints there was anything we, or anybody from the sixteenth century for that matter, would recognise as more than a very simple anchorage, but it does seem reasonable to suggest that the course of the Afon Col-huw followed a tidal inlet[5] at least 200 metres longer than at present, this creating a safer and more sheltered haven than the present geography suggests.

In addition, it is thought that the earliest monastery may have been situated to the south of the present town and near the confluence where the Hoddnant stream and the Ogney brook meet to form the mile-long river; this may have allowed small boats to approach quite close to the settlement. However, it would seem that by the ninth century the site was moved to where the current parish church still stands. The evidence for this is the presence of several inscribed stones and crosses (now beautifully housed in a small museum at the west end of the church) which date back to that time and appear to have been produced in what is now the churchyard, but which would once have been the community's *llan* and the site of a stonemason's workshop.

But arriving and departing from early Llantwit Major by means of the Bristol Channel presupposes a suitable vessel in which to do so. However, here archaeology is again helpful in showing the sea-going potential of boats in this period, with the notable example of the Barlands Farm boat being found not far away, near Newport (*Casnewydd*), in 1993.[6] At around eleven metres in length and about three metres across, this flat-bottomed vessel is thought to have been able to carry a cargo of about six tonnes. With a very sturdy frame of sawn oak timbers to which planks were attached with wooden nails, this boat would probably have had a single sail and a simple rudder, with its shallow draft making it ideal for the small inlets of the River Severn (*Afon Hafren*).

Dendrochronology dates the Barlands Farm boat to about 300 but, with the Romans not being accomplished boat builders themselves, it's thought that it is a good example of what native Celtic boatbuilding could achieve. Overall, it seems reasonable to assume that such skills persisted in succeeding centuries, enabling the sea-faring which is such an important factor in the history of this area.

The use of boats, though, requires safe and navigable routes and it's perhaps useful to note that the documentary evidence for the lost port at Llantwit Major includes mention of what seems to be a regular passage between there and the coast of

Somerset[7] and although only occasional pleasure trips are now made across the Bristol Channel, until quite recently there was frequent sea-borne trade across the water to ports such as Bideford and Barnstable.

The Saints' Way at Fowey, Cornwall

OS: SX 126 517

I came across the Saints' Way in Fowey, on the south coast of Cornwall, as I made my way to Brittany on my second pilgrimage,[8] with my overall aim being to increase my understanding of the links between this area of what is now western France and the shared Celtic culture of Cornwall and of Wales.

I arrived in Fowey from Polruan (*Porthruwan*) just over the estuary to the east, delighted to be making the short but very picturesque ferry crossing; this gave me an enjoyable break from walking and allowed me to see just a little of the sea-faring character of this greatly indented coastline.

It was also encouraging to come across a group of walkers from Germany who were happily exploring this beautiful area. I was able to chat with them for a while about my pilgrimage and pleased to be able to use my very patchy German to teach them, or perhaps just remind them, of a new word in English.

Having met the walking group twice on the Polruan side of the River Fowey (*Dowr Fowy*), I crossed over to the small town of the same name where I visited the impressive parish church of St Fimbarrus.[9] Later, sitting in the churchyard, two of the German hikers remembered me from earlier in the day and approached me to say hello again. It was lovely to be able to talk further with this couple, with one of them kindly going to get a takeaway coffee and a piece of cake for me.

It was at this point that I noticed a sign for the Saints' Way (*Forth an Syns*), the contemporary walking route that preserves the tradition, that the countryside between this area in the south of Cornwall and Padstow (*Lannwedhenek*) in the north of the county contains the course of an important ancient thoroughfare used by long-gone travellers.[10]

As I had arrived from the east, walking from the Plymouth area of Devon over the previous few days, I only intersected with the Saints' Way for a few miles as I continued on my way west to Polkerris (*Pollkerys*).[11] However, although the section of my pilgrimage following this waymarked trail was, on this occasion,[12] all too brief, it was intriguing to be in a place where journeys of so long ago are brought to mind in this twenty-seven mile route; for this is believed to be the way by which travellers from Wales, and also further afield from Ireland, traversed the Cornish peninsula in order to avoid the dangerous sea-crossing around Land's End (*Penn an Wlas*), before setting out for Brittany.

For me, at that time growing in my awareness of the importance of the sea as a means of travel, coming across the Saints' Way was clearly significant. This was not only in gaining a better understanding of the demands of such journeys and also the opportunities they provided, but also the means by which these are commemorated in our own time. It was certainly extraordinary to think that people on their way to and from Llantwit Major and other early Christian sites in south Wales fifteen hundred years ago, could have come through this same area of Cornwall where twenty-first century tourists, walkers and pilgrims still roam.

Of course, we can't be sure how accurately the contemporary Saints' Way represents the exact course taken by early medieval travellers, although as a walking trail, and publicised as such, it's still a great means to encourage an appreciation of the Celtic Christian heritage of Cornwall and beyond.

Meanwhile, St Michael's Way (*Fordh Sen Mighal*), which runs from Lelant (*Lannanta*) near St Ives (*Porth Ia*) to St Michael's Mount (*Karrek Loos yn Koos*) is promoted locally as

35

another very old route crossing Cornwall in the far west of the county.

The tomb of St Pompée, Langoat

0714 OT: 0238 6868

I visited the fine parish church at Langoat while walking along the Tro-Briez, making my way to the cathedral of St Tugdual at Tréguier.[13] Finding myself in a place of worship with many interesting artefacts, what particularly caught my eye that day was the large granite sarcophagus which marks the traditional burial place of St Pompée, Tugdual's mother.

In particular, I was touched to see that this thirteenth-century tomb depicts parent and son in a boat together.[14] It seemed so very human: perhaps a tale of protective filial love or even one of an adventurous older woman who shared her son's calling to the land across the sea. Now, the two are together for eternity in their small vessel shown in low-relief sculpture, together with a young child, thought to be a depiction of St Sève,[15] another of Pompée's children.

For this funerary monument – although belonging to a time about six hundred years after the original events – is a wonderful reminder of the voyages that are an essential element of the settlement of Brittany from Wales and the south-west of England between the fifth and seventh centuries. This is exemplified in the remarkable Breton tradition of the founder saints, of whom Tugdual is one, all of whom are thought to have had considerable connections with Britain, and specifically with Wales.[16]

However, there are no signs of any sailors to man the boat, with this seeming a little foreshortened to fit the proportions of the panel on the tomb where it's placed, but it is clearly similar to the Romano-Celtic boats such as found at Barlands. There is a sturdy prow, heavy overlapping timbers along the length and a central mast supported by rigging, where at least one sail could have powered them along on their missionary journey. For Tugdual holds his bishop's crozier firmly before him, whereas his mother carries what appears to be a book, surely representative of the Gospel that is to be proclaimed in the new land of Armorica, a territory whose very name indicates the all-importance of the sea.

For when Tugdual and his mother arrived by boat in what is now Brittany, they would have been travelling to what had formerly been part of the very large Roman province of Gallia Lugdenensis.[17] But the coastal area to which they sailed had already acquired the name of Armorica (*Arvorig*), derived from the Gaulish language (*are-mori* meaning 'at the sea'), such was the significance of the ocean at this place on the fringes of Western Europe.

For while we can't know for sure whether their voyage started in Wales or the south-west of England, they too may have taken the safe route by land between Fowey and Padstow, as I saw on my own travels so much later. However, they were bound for a place that had already experienced some planned settlement even in the Roman period with Britons, including those serving in the imperial army, being invited to settle in Armorica to stabilise the area against the incursions of the Frankish tribes to the east.

This process then seems to have continued, but perhaps on a greater scale, when the peoples known in English history as the Anglo-Saxons began to establish power bases in the south and east of England as imperial rule was withdrawn. A phenomenon which is much debated among historians, it appears to have set off a chain of events which spread, albeit slowly, over to the west of what had been *Britannia*. There, some inhabitants of what is now Wales and the south-west of England – regions already seeing migration from Ireland – appear to have been displaced and sought to migrate to Armorica.

This new land was presumably an attractive destination, perhaps being relatively peaceful and maybe sparsely populated.

It was clearly also in quite close proximity and with what must have been some cultural similarities.[18]And although we have no idea of the numbers involved, they appear to have been sufficient to mark the new land as 'little Britain' and to cause the language spoken there to evolve closer to Brittonic, which would, over the next few centuries, diversify into early Welsh, Cornish and Breton.[19] Interestingly, the latter has developed to be particularly close to Cornish rather than Welsh, which implies that those who settled in Brittany from the south-west of England were in the majority among the migrants. This theory also seems to be supported by the existence in Brittany of the area known as Dumnonée (*Domnonea*), this being derived from *Dumnonia*, the Roman name for south-west England.

Overall, though, there is still a lot to be learnt about the process of settlement in Brittany. In addition, there is also the observation that some higher status individuals, presumably a minority as the linguistic evidence suggests, seem to have had stronger connections with Wales rather than the West Country. This has then led to speculation as to how far church-planting in the south-west of England was due to outside influences, notably from Wales but also from Ireland, and how far it was indigenous and home-grown.

And although Tugdual, together with his mother and sister, would have been part of the wider migration, the kingly lineage spoken of in his *Vitae* is especially interesting in that he appears to already have had family ties in their new home. Thus, it seems likely that the existing connections of some of the more aristocratic settlers helped them to integrate into society in Brittany, and in particular receive the all-important grants of land on which to build churches.

All in all, it's perhaps not surprising that this period of history was so formative of Brittany, as we see it even today, although it must be remembered that the region was already at least nominally Christian when the newcomers set ashore.

Like Wales, the new faith may have arrived as early as the third century, but it would appear that beyond Roman centres such as Rennes (*Roazhon*), the ordinary people of the countryside remained largely beyond the reach of the church at this time.[20] As regards sources for what we know about Tugdual, there are three *Vitae* in existence, believed to have been written in the sixth, ninth and eleventh centuries respectively. The first and last of these both place his birth in Britain, with the writer of the eleventh-century work, which was almost certainly written at Tréguier, at pains to point out that the belief expressed in the second *Vita* that Tugdual came from Ireland is erroneous.[21] What this discrepancy highlights, though, is not only the very mobile lifestyle of men such Tugdual, who is likely to have studied in Ireland, but also the lack of any notion of what we would call nationality.

Meanwhile Tugdual lives on in the many place-names in Brittany that are believed to be derived from his name and which may mark the site of early churches which he, or his followers, founded. However, trying to deduce some historical facts about him through this means is complicated, not only by there being many variants of his name, such as Tudal and Tutuarn, but that he appears to have had an alternative name, Pabu, which is also found in various forms.

However, back in Wales there are only two places associated with him, that is the St Tudwal's Islands (*Ynysoedd Tudwal*) off the coast of the Llŷn peninsula, where he may have lived for a while as a hermit,[22] and also the church dedicated to Tudwal at Llanstadwell (*Llanudwal*), which is on the north bank of the River Cleddau (*Afon Cleddau*) near Milford Haven (*Aberdaugleddau*) in Pembrokeshire (*Sir Benfro*). Both very suitable, watery places for this saint, forever on his voyage across the sea with his mother and sister.

CHAPTER 3

On a tiny island and excursions to the Wirral and the Isle of Man

THIS CHAPTER FOCUSES on a small island and the saint who may have sought it as a place of seclusion and prayer; a medieval parish church just over the border from Wales on the Wirral in north-west England; and a large and historic churchyard on the Isle of Man. With each of these contrasting places being interesting to visit, they also all help us appreciate how much there is still to learn. This is particularly the case for the centuries between the end of the Roman occupation and about 800.

Of course, Wales is well-known for the very considerable number of early saints who are associated with the dedications of its parish churches; and however difficult it may seem to track them down today, these are generally considered to have been actual people rather than legendary characters. Moreover, they vary hugely from those with many dedications, the supreme example here being St David (with over fifty in south Wales), to those with just one, such as St Ilan (and here the name may have arisen due to confusion with *llan*), as at Eglwysilan near Caerphilly (*Caerffili*). The written evidence for these people is also varied, but one thing they share is that none of the Welsh saints of this period has left us with any writings of their own. Instead, other people, usually much later, wrote about them (but by no means all) in their *Vitae*, often seeming to have taken material from pre-existing sources to produce works which can be difficult for us to decipher today.

Some of the saints also appear not only in early genealogies and so on, but also in later medieval poetry. In addition, many of their names have become attached to features in the landscape, notably springs of water which have become known as 'holy wells'.

However, in the first section of this chapter, I have chosen to focus on St Tysilio who has six churches, an island and a poem dedicated to him. This is followed by looking at the topic of circular churchyards, although in the context of English post-war housing rather than rural Wales as might be expected. The chapter concludes with a trip to the Isle of Man to look at how some early Christian sites seem to have evolved to include several chapels or churches in one large enclosure.

St Tysilio built this church, 630 AD

OS: SH 551 717

St Tysilio's Church at Menai Bridge (*Porthaethwy*) is one of several churches on small islands that can be found along the coast of the bigger island of Anglesey (*Ynys Môn*), situated off the coast of north Wales.[1] Built on what is little more than a rocky outcrop and with several even smaller islets close by, St Tysilio's may have originated as a hermitage where isolation was relieved twice every day as the tide on the Menai Strait (*Afon Menai*) receded.

The day that I discovered this delightful spot, I had walked from the town of Bethesda, well known for its huge slate quarries, through the cathedral city of Bangor and then on to Anglesey following the Wales Coast Path. Tucked away just a short distance from Thomas Telford's Menai Suspension Bridge (*Pont Grog y Borth*),[2] it was wonderful to come across Church Island (*Ynys Tysilio*) at the end of its own short causeway: this provides access not only to St Tysilio's Church but also to the nearby war memorial. On the landward side of the causeway, The Belgian Promenade (*Rhodfa'r Belgiaid*), constructed in gratitude by refugees during the Great War, adds to the historical interest of this place.[3]

Although a picturesque and clearly very useful feature today, the history of the causeway is uncertain. There is no indication of it on John Speed's map of 1611, whereas Mercator's map of about 1619 clearly shows such an approach to the island, although apparently coming from the northward shore rather than from the east as is the case with the causeway in its current position.[4]

However, what really intrigued me at Church Island was the bold statement on a faded but still very prominent notice above the door declaring: 'St Tysilio Built this Church, 630 AD.' Although plenty of Welsh churches make a claim to an ancient foundation I have never, before or since, seen such confident belief expressed with so much conviction.

But, what do we know about Tysilio and what is there to connect him to this dot of land off the coast of Anglesey?

Like many early saints, Tysilio is thought to have been of royal descent, being the son of Brochwel Ysgythrog, king of Powys. Although today the name of Wales' largest county, at that time Powys was a small kingdom in what is now north-east Wales. However, it also extended into what would later become Mercia and eventually part of England, with Brochwel's seat of power likely to have been in the area of what is now Shrewsbury (*Amwythig*).

Active in the late sixth and early seventh century, we can learn of Tysilio from a twelfth-century poem written in his honour by Cynddelw Brydydd Mawr,[5] then a court poet to the kings of Powys, who also claimed descent from Brochwel Ysgythrog, thus making the saint their distant kinsman. Although this ode very much reflects the context in which it was written and contains little real information about him, it reflects the veneration in which Tysilio was held and his perceived significance in the history of the kingdom.

But, apart from a brief mention in the fourteenth-century *Life of St Beuno*, the main source for what we know of Tysilio is a fifteenth-century *Life of Suliac* written in Brittany to provide a history of the founding of the church at St-Suliac.[6] The writers of this document appear to have had access to an earlier *Vita* circulating in the region at the time and, with the similarities of the two names, it may be the case that some reasonably reliable information about Tysilio has been preserved in this way.

However, an additional complication, at least as far as the reliability of the story as regards the beginnings of the church at St-Suliac is concerned, is that our Tysilio is probably not the same person as the Suliac whose memory the writers intended to preserve.

But the Breton *Life of Suliac*, assuming this contains some genuine information about Tysilio, corroborates his royal ancestry[7] and tells us that Tysilio wished to follow a religious life, leading him to settle for some time in Meifod to receive instruction from the founder and abbot, Gwyddfarch. His sojourn on Anglesey, at what we know as Church Island, then followed on from this but he then left for Brittany to escape the demand of his widowed sister-in-law that he should marry her. To the writers of the Breton *Vita*, this was the point when he founded the church at St-Suliac.

To further complicate Tysilio's story, there may be not two but even three people of a similar name, and involving conflated histories, not only in Brittany and north Wales but also in the south-west of England. However, one possibility is that St Sulien, the founder-abbot of the church in the Cornish village of Luxulyan (*Logsulyan*), might be the same person as St Suliac, which would at least lessen the confusion!

Back in Wales, there remains the issue of the other churches dedicated to Tysilio and how the scattered nature

43

of these places might be explained. At Meifod, it seems that the original dedication was to the founder Gwyddfarch, with Tysilio later superseding him because of his connections with the royal house as exemplified in Cynddelw's poem. Three further dedications to the north of Meifod probably also reflect his place as a saint of Powys whose cult remained important in the area in the post-Norman period; as new churches were founded it would appear that Tysilio was taken as the patron.

However, there are also two outlying dedications in south-west Wales at Llandysul and Llandissilio. One explanation is that, if Tysilio did travel south to Brittany, these may be places where he founded a simple chapel along the way which then became venerated by local people with his name attached to it. However, they could just be evidence of travel within Wales or of his name being taken much later for reasons unknown to us.

There is also one parish church dedicated to Tysilio in Herefordshire, where the village of Sellack derives its name from Suluc, a variant of Tysilio. Sellack is situated within what was known as Archenfield (*Ergyng*), a small Celtic kingdom which retained some independence even into the Norman period. As such, the dedication to Tysilio is just one of many to Celtic saints in an area where connections with Wales remain very strong. At Sellack there is no way of knowing if this indicates a church actually founded by Tysilio, or that a later dedication took his name which also then evolved into the name of the village. There is also just a suggestion that the original dedication at Titley, near Kington and also in Herefordshire, was to Tysilio.

Meanwhile, what can we learn about the extraordinary story of the early saints in Wales from what we know about Tysilio, and how typical is he of a Welsh saint of these centuries?

Tysilio's royal lineage and his determination to follow a religious life are common themes in the lives of many saints, both men and women. His desire to seek seclusion, as exemplified by his island hermitage at Church Island, and his rejection of his sister-in-law's advances and the kingly power this would have given him, are also similar to the traditions surrounding other early religious figures. Tysilio also clearly went on to be remembered and venerated many centuries later, with his story extending over to Brittany even if his real travels may not have actually taken him there.

Holy Cross Church, Woodchurch, Wirral

OS: SJ 276 868

There is a pervasive belief that circular churchyards indicate somewhere that has been used as a place of Christian worship since the earliest times, when a missionary monk or local saint enclosed a parcel of land and instituted a simple church there. This is often combined with a suggestion that the curved shape may represent continuity of design with a wider Celtic culture or that the place concerned may have been associated with pre-Christian pagan practices. There are lots of examples of this type of thinking, whether in contemporary guides to churches or in older antiquarian texts.[8]

Like many people interested in old churches and ancient religious sites, I too find myself intrigued when I come across yet another circular, or perhaps put more accurately, *curvilinear* Welsh churchyard. For there is no doubting that there are almost countless examples in Wales, as well as in other areas of western Britain and beyond. In the county of Powys alone there are believed to be over seventy such churchyards.

However, I'd like to start with considering the example of the Holy Cross Church at Woodchurch on the Wirral, not far from the border with Flintshire (*Sir y Fflint*). I came across this fascinating place as I walked north on pilgrimage to the Isle of Man.

Hoping to attend a Sunday morning service and aware from reading my map that I would be going into a very built-up area, I made my way through a country park and passed a major hospital before crossing a busy road and turning into a large housing estate. All in all, I would have to admit that these things had the effect of making me look out for a modern-style church, which I was anticipating would also be in a tarmac car park and probably looking rather dreary too. How wrong I would be proven to be!

I was looking out for such a church, but failing to see it, when I became aware that I was walking on a curved section of road bounded by a wall and with trees and shrubs beyond. So different was this to what I had expected, I wondered whether I had taken the wrong turn. It then took a few seconds for me to realise that my route was taking me around a curvilinear enclosure. In addition, I noticed that the ground level within was considerably higher than that of the pavement I was walking on and the road alongside, a feature that often accompanies such spaces.

A few metres on, I saw the lychgate marking the entrance to the churchyard with what was clearly a medieval church within it. As if to complete this very serendipitous moment, a couple of people at the lychgate noticed me approaching and beckoned me towards them in welcome. This marked the beginning of an extraordinary morning at Holy Cross which was not only followed by a kind invitation to Sunday lunch but also a request that I visit the church again on my way home from the Isle of Man.

Coming across the curvilinear churchyard at Holy Cross was so surprising to me because I had not expected anything like it in such an urban area, although I would have to admit that if I had examined my map more closely I might have suspected something, particularly on the east side of the churchyard – the boundary of an early church enclosure survives from a very different age. To this day, it remains perhaps the most memorable of all such churchyards I have come across in my walking.

Later that morning, some of the friendly congregation

at Holy Cross were keen to answer my questions, telling me that the church had been surrounded by fields until after the Second World War, when a large area of new housing was built, rapidly transforming the area but leaving the church and its curvilinear graveyard in the south-western segment of this development.[9]

It was also explained to me that nearby Landican,[10] a hamlet less than a mile away and consisting of a farm and a few cottages, was believed to be a Welsh-style place-name derived from the days when this area was still Brittonic-speaking. As such, it would be related to the many 'llan' and 'lan' place-names not only in Wales, Cornwall and Brittany, but also in other outliers such as Lancaut in Gloucestershire.[11]

But what is the provenance of curvilinear churchyards such as at Woodchurch as regards to how old they may be and what reasons can be given for the curving shape?

Unfortunately for the attractive idea of the historicity of what are often very picturesque spaces, there is very little evidence that such enclosures in themselves indicate a church site that goes back to the early medieval period or to the Age of the Saints. However, it does seem likely that such shapes may well have originated when the enclosure was the first made in what was then a largely open landscape, but it does not of itself prove anything as regards the approximate date of the enclosure.[12]

There is also the very practical consideration that, if you were to fell trees and clear scrub from a fixed point, you are likely to create a clearing with a rounded perimeter.[13] In addition, it could be proposed that if earthen banks were surmounted by a simple timber palisade, which appears to have often been the case, such a superstructure would lend itself to a curved shape far more than modern construction techniques with walls and fences do.

Another possibility is that the circular nature of so many churchyards is a result of the development of laws relating to sanctuary, whereby those accused of crime could escape hasty judgements and perhaps summary execution by placing themselves within the protection provided on church land. This practice seems to have developed from about the eighth century in Wales and it may be that the number of paces from a fixed point within which the sanctuary applied could be reflected in some of the examples of curvilinear churchyards which have survived into our own times. Double enclosures, which can also be seen in some places, may also reflect perhaps the bounds of sanctuary in addition to an inner church enclosure proper.[14]

Meanwhile, another interesting curvilinear feature that I have come across is that at St Peter's church in Stanton Lacy in Shropshire. There, within the current bounds of the churchyard following its expansion in the later medieval period, can clearly be seen the curved bank of an earlier enclosure. Dated by some to the sixth century (although I have been unable to find any corroboration of this), it is presumably the earliest enclosure here.[15] Unfortunately, the bank has at some time been lost on its northern side to a neighbouring farmyard, but it remains a notable sight. It is also a reminder, as is Holy Cross at Woodchurch, that curvilinear churchyards would also have been a feature of the landscape in what is now England and are not a specifically Welsh phenomenon.

Kirk Maughold, Isle of Man

OS: SC 496 917

I was taken to Kirk Maughold when I had an opportunity to visit as part of the *Praying the Keeills* annual festival on the Isle of Man. Those of us gathered there that morning were able to enjoy a guided tour around this historic and extensive four-acre site close to the north-east coast. This includes not only the church itself but also the remains of several ancient chapels or *keeills* and, perhaps most impressive of all, the memorial stones and crosses that are housed under a shelter in the churchyard. This collection contains some splendid examples, including one known as Guriat's Cross (derived from the inscription *crux guriat*) which is believed to date from the ninth century.

However, one of the things that really struck me that day was the large size of the churchyard and the number and variety of the features within it. With interesting input from some of the festival team, I was able to learn something of the accounts of how Christianity may have come to the island and the possible significance in that process of what is still the home of an active church.

St Patrick of Ireland is traditionally seen as the one who first brought the Christian faith to Mann, but it is uncertain as to whether he ever really set foot on the island. However, the twelfth-century *Life of Patrick* by Jocelin of Furness[16] portrays a cruel tyrant with the Latinised name of Machaldus who, when confronted with the holiness of Patrick, repents of his evil ways and in great contrition of spirit allows himself to be put to sea to be led where God wills him to go. Not content with his little boat having no oars or rudder, Machaldus agrees to his legs being locked in shackles. Eventually he comes to shore on Mann where two holy men find the key to his bonds in the mouth of a fish. They befriend Machaldus, who joins them in their life of ministering to the local people, eventually carrying on their work after they die.[17]

Jocelin of Furness' main source for his *Life of Patrick* would have been an earlier *Vita* of the saint written by Muirchu, a monk in Armagh in the late seventh century,[18] but it isn't clear in this text that Maccuil, as Muirchu names the cruel tyrant in his text, really is the same person as Machaldus (or Maughold) or even if the island where he finally comes ashore is Mann. Unfortunately, it is possible that Jocelin of Furness took the earlier *Vita* and used it as a source simply on the basis of a slight similarity between the two names. But as with all these very early stories, it's hard to imagine that there isn't a kernel of truth to be found somewhere.

Meanwhile, the complexities surrounding Jocelin's account of the arrival of Machaldus on Mann, to say nothing of the role of Patrick and the two men already ministering on the island, are many. However, the story of a penitent tyrant arriving in his little boat after drifting across the Irish Sea is certainly a rather attractive one, and depictions of the saint in his coracle without oars are seen in many places on the island.

Fortunately for Kirk Maughold, though, and anyone who takes an interest in this place, the ancient memorial stones and crosses associated with the churchyard and the surrounding area provide a much clearer witness to the history of the site than either Jocelin of Furness or Muirchu of Armagh.

This extensive collection, protected from the elements in the Maughold Cross House constructed in 1906, includes forty-five pieces of which many were found in the churchyard or close by. However, for our purposes in considering the origins of Kirk Maughold as an early ecclesiastical site on Mann, the oldest stones are clearly especially relevant as they include cross slabs which have been dated to about the seventh century. Together, they are good evidence for the establishment of Maughold as a religious centre in the pre-Norse period on the island.[19]

For although the stone monuments may not quite take us back as far as the time of St Patrick, or in any way endorse the story of Machaldus and his coracle, they make it quite reasonable for us to believe that this place was the site of an early Christian settlement. As such, it would have been almost certainly a simple monastery with a variety of small buildings built in some combination of wood, thatch, wattle and daub. No evidence of these structures has survived, but a hint as to their existence may perhaps be found in the remains of the three *keeills*, which are still such a feature at Maughold.

These can be seen above ground (a fourth being marked only by a cross) and are believed to date from several centuries after the foundation of the monastery. Orientated roughly east to west and now visible as low stone walls and considerably landscaped and restored, they are thought to be from the Norse period on Mann between the tenth and twelfth centuries. Excavated by P.M.C. Kermode, the great antiquarian and historian of the island, between 1911 and 1914, these simple chapels were found to include evidence of stone altars and features such as porches, with the North Keeill even having its own small graveyard around it.[20]

Of course, the *keeills* as we see them now are not thought to have necessarily been in the same position as the earlier pre-Norse buildings that would have been their predecessors, but the survival of this number of *keeills* within the churchyard speaks of the site's beginnings as a monastery in the Age of the Saints, with these structures perhaps having their antecedents in mortuary chapels of key figures in its distant past. As such, they are an intriguing reminder of Maughold's development into a small monastic city, a distant cousin of the great examples in Ireland, such as Glendalough.

The current church is also a survivor of those times, in that it too has evolved from an earlier *keeill*.[21] By the eleventh century, it is known to have been a parish church, with this role being adopted around the time of a more formal bishopric being instituted on the island as a consequence of Norman settlement on Mann. This would also have marked the end, presuming it was still in existence, of the older monastery, as such places made way for religious houses on a continental model.[22] On Mann, this was at Rushen Abbey which was a Savignac and then Cistercian house and a daughter establishment of the abbey at Furness, home to our friend Jocelin. It was also at around this time that the church may have been dedicated to St Olaf, the martyr-king of Norway.

Although the church was much restored in early twentieth century, remnants of the twelfth-century Romanesque phase of building on the site can be seen in a few surviving fragments. These include a handsome capital with an animal face, apparently of a bear, and circular patterns carved in sandstone, now in the Manx Museum in Douglas.

The church also now houses the splendid medieval churchyard cross which dates from about 1300.[23] This is a unique survivor on Mann and one of the best examples still in existence in the British Isles.

Clearly Kirk Maughold stands as a remarkable testimony to the monastery that existed on this site perhaps as early as the sixth century, and the work of mission and evangelisation that would have been conducted from it. Of course, the monastery would have evolved and changed as a mirror of the developments on Mann as a whole, with the variety of artistic styles found on the stone monuments witnessing to the many influences from near and far. It would also seem reasonable to assume that Kirk Maughold was continuously occupied, as the number of surviving stone monuments and the wide range of dates to which these can be attributed to make it likely that it never fell out of use.

As such, it is clearly significant in Manx history, but perhaps Kirk Maughold has a wider role in helping us to better appreciate how similar places existed in Wales, even if they are now rather less obvious than what can be seen here on the Isle of Man.

At Meifod, already discussed earlier in this chapter, we have perhaps the closest example to Kirk Maughold in Wales. With one of the largest churchyards in the country, not only does a twelfth-century document appear to record the existence of two churches on the site, but a chapel associated with a graveyard is also believed to have stood at a point now outside the boundary as it exists today. And Meifod is not alone, in that it is known that there were formerly two medieval churches (dedicated to St Tudclyd and to St Enclydwyn) within the churchyard at Penmachno, with the present Victorian building being on the site of one of them.

There may not be a monastic foundation of the scale and complexity of Kirk Maughold to see in Wales but, with its several *keeills* and a considerable collection of ancient inscribed stones, this Manx churchyard can certainly help us better appreciate how an early religious settlement may have looked so many centuries ago.

CHAPTER 4

For the price
of my best horse

THE PREVIOUS CHAPTER was mainly concerned with people and places. In a culture where there was little if any concept of private ownership, land was gifted by the elite of the time in order to provide a site for religious use. This process was fundamental to the growing use of legal charters to regulate the new situation whereby land was being alienated, to use the technical term.

Meanwhile, the Church was also acquiring what might be called a professional class, that is, of clerics under some form of vows. This group is generally, for the sake of simplicity, described as saints, although missionary monks and itinerant holy men (there are few women among them) might be helpful alternatives. However, in addition to these developments, churches also began to acquire artefacts which were used in Christian worship and in the context of the small communities within which the early saints are generally believed to have lived.

This chapter discusses three such items that have survived from the early medieval period and what we can learn from them. This involves not only the technology and skills used in their making, but also the place of these items – a bell, a Gospel Book, and a very modest socket stone – in the context of churches and religious practice in Wales and further afield.

St Gwyddelan's Bell, Dolwyddelan

OS: SH 736 523

I arrived in Dolwyddelan, in the Snowdonia area of north Wales, after some problematic walking. What can only be described as 'extreme mud' had made it necessary to repeatedly make minor detours away from the 'other route with public access' that had looked so straightforward on my map. I was then concerned that I might lose my way altogether if I wandered too far from where I was supposed to be.

Several streams to ford also added to the adventure although a couple of place-names on the map, *Pigyn Esgob* (bishop's thorn) and *Bwlch y Groes* (pass of the cross) helped me to appreciate that, however difficult things were, I was perhaps not the first pilgrim to pass that way.

However, having finally arrived in Dolwyddelan, the charm and interest of this village more than made up for the obstacles I'd experienced, although, at first, it seemed a little incongruous to be in a place with a major road going through it, a shop and also a railway station. But I was soon to come across perhaps the most extraordinary artefact, outside of a museum, that I have ever seen on any of my pilgrimages: St Gwyddelan's bell (*Cloch Gwyddelan*). The bell's home, the local parish church, has an information board which instructs visitors as follows: 'In the centre aisle, if you look up you will see an old Celtic bell hanging from the beam. It was dug up in 1850 on the site of the original church.'

Although I was already aware of the existence in Wales of some early medieval bells, I was delighted to discover the well-preserved example here in Dolwyddelan. Going into the church, I peered up towards the roof to see it safely suspended high above the nave.

Looking rather like a big cow-bell, St Gwyddelan's bell is quadrangular in shape and, measuring about 30cm in height and 20cm in width, its size is typical of these extraordinary items. Moreover, the bell is one of only six ecclesiastical hand

55

bells to have survived from the pre-Norman period in Wales. Like all the others bar one, the bell was cast in copper alloy, and was found within the ancient Welsh kingdom of Gwynedd.[1]

The exception among the Welsh bells as regards both location and material is the one found in the eighteenth century in Llangenny (*Llangenau*) in the Black Mountains (*Y Mynyddoedd Duon*) of south Wales. This was made of iron, which was then coated with copper alloy in a process known as brazing.[2] Moreover, across Ireland, Scotland and Wales, where a total of over a hundred bells are still in existence, brazed iron bells, such as at Llangenny, considerably outnumber those cast from copper alloy, which makes the ratio among surviving Welsh bells exceptional and, as yet, unexplained.[3]

What is perhaps encouraging, though, about the Dolwyddelan bell is that it was quite unknown until the mid-nineteenth century when it was dug up at nearby Bryn y Bedd, which was the site of the parish church until the late fifteenth century.[4] This 'hill of the grave' is only about four hundred metres from the current church, which was built by Maredudd ab Ieuan who lived at the local castle. An ancestor of the well-known Wynn family of this area of north Wales, Maredudd seems to have hoped that rebuilding the church in its current position would give greater protection from the outlaws who were, at that time, creating problems in the area.[5]

Bryn y Bedd may have been the site of a succession of churches, from a simple wooden structure in the Age of the Saints to the last one constructed there, in stone, in the early twelfth century. Moreover, the name may indicate that it was the burial place of the original founder of the church. By tradition this is St Gwyddelan, who is thought to have come from Ireland perhaps as early as the fifth century. With his name meaning 'the little Irishman', the place-name of the village as a whole denotes the 'meadow of the little Irishman'.

However, although a leading authority has commented that 'it would look at home in Ireland',[6] St Gwyddelan's bell is not now thought to have been brought to the area by the little Irishman himself, but sometime later. As the bell would have been a prized object and associated with the abbot of a monastery, it would seem reasonable to claim that Bryn y Bedd was the place of a small, early Christian community, with a later leader in the eighth or ninth century probably bringing the bell over from Ireland. With the production of these types of copper alloy bells becoming more widespread by this time, this chronology as to the arrival of the bell in Dolwyddelan seems to better fit what we know of the evolution of bell-casting techniques.

As to its purpose, the bell would have been used to mark the time of prayer, to summon people to worship, and have been rung during the liturgy as still happens in Roman Catholic and some Anglican churches today. Gazing up at the bell that day was an extraordinary reminder, not only of the religious rites in which it would have played a part but, in addition, the simple, practical need to make the community aware that a time of worship or prayer was about to be observed.

It may also have been associated with funeral rites and the displaying of relics on the anniversary of the founder's death

Early medieval bells are believed to be derived from small handbells used in the Roman Empire. These were for domestic and temple use and were similar to cow bells which were also in existence by this time. Like many of the early medieval church bells which appear to be their successors, Roman bells were made of iron, with it being possible that the technology to make them was imitated in post-Roman Wales from where it reached Ireland. This itself could have been alongside the process of Christianisation in Ireland which, although our understanding remains incomplete, appears to have involved at least some mission from Wales.

Once in use in Ireland, and with Christian communities there growing in wealth and influence, bells seem to have been manufactured on a considerable scale. Notably, excavation close to an early church site at Clonfad in County Westmeath has provided archaeological evidence for the making of a large number of iron bells from approximately the sixth to the ninth century.[7]

However, there is a lack of evidence, in either Ireland or Wales, for similar large-scale production of bells in cast copper alloy as at Dolwyddelan. This suggests that they may have been manufactured by itinerant craftsmen. Also, the lack of shared but distinguishing characteristics among the surviving examples in north Wales implies that they are not a group which was the work of a single person or a particular workshop. In all, it would seem reasonable to assume, as appears to be the case at Dolwyddelan, that they may each have been brought over from Ireland in separate circumstances, although manufacture within Wales cannot be ruled out. [8]

Further afield, the few examples that remain in Brittany may have been taken there from Wales and the south-west of England and are likely to be material evidence for the early settlement of Brittany from these regions, as discussed earlier in chapter two.[9]

St Gwyddelan's bell is certainly an extraordinary artefact which we're very fortunate to be able to see today in a situation not too far removed in place and purpose from where it would have been in ninth-century Eryri. The current parish church certainly provides a lovely setting for it.

About a mile to the west of the village, Dolwyddelan Castle can also be visited, with its elevated position providing splendid views towards the mountains not far away. Meanwhile, in the car park of a local hotel, there's information about the holy well *Ffynnon Sant Gwyddelan*, the English name for which is given as 'Elen's Well'. This probably derives from a misunderstanding of the final syllable of the village's name and has led to various alternative accounts of the origin of the place-name and who Elen may have been.

Unfortunately, access to the well, which is on private

property, remains difficult and I wasn't able to see it that day. However, it remains as another possible glimpse into historic Dolwyddelan, 'the meadow of the little Irishman'.

The Llandeilo Gospels Exhibition

OS: SN 629 222

The Llandeilo Gospel Book is something that I have come across in two places and two very different formats. As such it is unique among the many things I have seen as I walked, with both versions speaking powerfully of the age in which they were made, one being a priceless illuminated manuscript and the other being the same document in a pioneering digital form.[10]

The first time I was able to see the Llandeilo Gospel Book was in the digital format in which it can be viewed in the town in south-west Wales from which it takes one of its many names. There, the local church of St Teilo is home to a small visitor centre, known as the Llandeilo Gospels Exhibition, where information about the Gospel Book and the times in which it was written is available not only on display boards but also on several interactive screens. These also allow you to look at the manuscript itself, turning the pages as you go as if you were reading a real book.[11]

This first opportunity to see the Gospel Book was when I was making my way back from Glendalough in the Wicklow Hills and heading for home. Having taken the ferry from Ireland to Pembroke Dock (*Doc Penfro*), I needed to cross south Wales from west to east. Taking a route which gave me a few days on the beautiful coast path, I then roughly followed the route of the A40 road from Carmarthen, which then brought me to Llandeilo.

However, the experience of being able to view the Gospel Book in the visitor centre that day, to say nothing of the additional information available, encouraged me to consider whether a future pilgrimage might include the historic cathedral at Lichfield, home to the *real* Gospel Book for the last thousand years or so; for what I saw that day in Llandeilo was only a copy, albeit a sophisticated one, of the genuine article.

It was to be two years before I finally arrived in Lichfield on pilgrimage and was able to see this original and precious artefact in the chapter house of the cathedral. There too, the Gospel Book was displayed, although to very different effect from Llandeilo, with it being open at a page containing only text and enclosed within a glass case.

With several pages containing beautiful illuminated work, I have to say that I felt a little disappointed that what was on view at Lichfield only featured script rather than the vivid illustrations I had hoped I would see.[12] I can only assume that one of these plainer pages had been chosen because of the risk of deterioration once the pigments used are exposed to modern electric light. All in all, it was certainly a rather different experience of the book to the one I had previously had in Wales, where I had been able to leaf through its pages, albeit in a virtual way.

As at Llandeilo though, some information was provided to explain the importance of the Gospel Book and, in particular, its place in the history of Lichfield Cathedral. What is on view there is thought to be the survivor of a two-volume set which would have originally included all the four New Testament gospels.[13] However, only the Gospels of Matthew, Mark and the early chapters of the Gospel of Luke are still in existence today, all bound together relatively recently within thin boards of oak which replicate the original early medieval binding. Dating to first half of the eighth century, the Gospel Book is a notable example of the book production techniques of the time, although it would have to be admitted that it is inferior in design and execution to the perhaps better-known *Lindisfarne Gospels* and the *Book of Kells*.[14]

But what can be seen both as an actual document in Lichfield and a digital one in Llandeilo goes under many different names and, having chosen to refer to it here in a general way as a 'Gospel Book', I made a deliberate choice to use a non-controversial and perhaps rather bland term. However, I started this section with just one of its many names, 'The Llandeilo Gospel Book', not least because it was in this west Wales town that I first came across it.

But why does this extraordinary volume go under so many different names?

To some extent this is just to do with preference and convention, but it is also related to the discussions, verging on disputes, that surround it.

On the one hand, some names given to the book include references to Lichfield and its founder and patron, the Anglo-Saxon churchman St Chad (d. 672), while others connect it with Teilo, the sixth-century saint of Llandeilo, which is also thought to be the site of his burial and shrine. As a result, the volume goes under terms varying from 'The Lichfield Gospels' and 'The St Chad Gospels' to 'St Teilo's Gospels' and 'The Llandeilo Fawr Gospels', as well as even more variants for an artefact whose curious wanderings have implications for Welsh history and culture even in our own times. In short, these names highlight the competing claims of Llandeilo and Lichfield to be the book's true home.

Some of the history of the Gospel Book is, fortunately, uncontroversial, although still much discussed. This includes the remarkable words, contained within the book itself, that it was placed 'on the altar of holy Teilo' having been purchased by a man named Gelhi 'for the price of his best horse'. Written in Latin as a marginal note following the custom of the time, this is believed to refer to a transaction resulting in the Gospel Book being donated to the church at Llandeilo.[15] With the gift being witnessed by someone named as Cincenn, it is thought that the death of this person's father is recorded in the Annals of Wales (*Annales Cambriae*) as having occurred in

814, thus providing reasonable evidence for the book being in Llandeilo in the early ninth century. Related to this issue is the possibility that 'the altar of holy Teilo' could refer to what is now the cathedral at Llandaff (*Llandaf*) with which Teilo also became associated (and remains a patron). However, as other *marginalia* (which have great importance as being among the earliest examples of written Welsh) have been shown to deal with places close to Llandeilo, it is now thought that this is the location where the book was handed over.

The acquisition by Gelhi of the Gospel Book in what are clearly very irregular circumstances remains intriguing, not least in considering how the vendor had acquired it; for it would have been an item of considerable value in every sense of the word and not something that its original owners would have relinquished or put on the open market, as we might say.

The implication has to be that the book had been stolen and the person offering it to Gelhi – for what would have been the modest price of a horse, albeit the purchaser's best one – was in possession of it without any reasonable entitlement to it. One can only imagine that Gelhi saw his buying of the book as an act of piety or even of penitence, restoring it to its rightful place within a Christian community.

But where did the vendor get the book, and could there have been several middlemen in its story before it finally got into Gelhi's hands?

As is often the case with this period of history, the Vikings may have been the original culprits, with raids in the early ninth century in Northumbria and Ireland. With the riches of early medieval monasteries often in their sights, it would seem reasonable to suggest that the Gospel Book was Viking plunder that then found its way back among the native population perhaps by being 'ransomed'.

However, this leads to several competing theories and claims about where the book was originally copied, with the concomitant need for a high level of skill and expertise, as well as access to valuable materials. It is in this aspect that the discussions surrounding the Gospel Book become more heated.

Fortunately, the Latin used in the text is some help in that it uses a form of the fourth-century Vulgate translation (from the original Greek of the New Testament) which is known from other early manuscripts to have been in use at several monasteries within the Anglo-Saxon kingdom of Northumbria or those associated with them. The case for a Northumbrian origin is also supported by the style of some of the illustrations, notably the interlaced birds on the cross-carpet page which are very similar to a design seen on a cross fragment found at Aberlady in the south of Scotland.[16]

However, the monasteries suggested by the distinctive Latin of the text also include some religious houses within the kingdom of Mercia, whose foundations were also related to Northumbria. It is this possible origin within Mercia, and more particularly at Lichfield, which is promoted at the cathedral today. There, in the information provided for visitors, the Gospel Book is portrayed as having returned to its true home.

Recent archaeological discoveries also seem to support the case for Lichfield having been the place where the book was made. These include the use of motifs similar to those found in metalwork in the Anglo-Saxon treasures known as the Staffordshire Hoard.[17]

More significant, though, is perhaps the Lichfield Angel, a stone fragment thought to have been part of the earliest shrine to Chad. This was probably built around the time of the construction of the first cathedral on the site in about 700, with some surviving pigment on the angel being the same distinctive hue as one used in the book's illuminated text; with the angel having been found during archaeological work on the nave of the cathedral in 2003, it is now displayed alongside the Gospel Book.[18]

But Wales can also be considered to have a claim to be

the place where the book may have been produced, with the scriptorium of the monastery at Llanbadarn Fawr being seen by some as possibly having scribes with the appropriate level of skill. Associated with this theory is the similarity of the text with that of the Hereford Gospels, which remain to this day in the famous chained library at the cathedral in the city. As a claim is made for the Hereford Gospels to be a product of a Welsh religious house, could the Gospel Book also possibly have been made in Wales?[19]

All of this is tinged with ongoing discussion and debate as to what we know of eighth-century Wales and its capacity to produce such a book, with this being accentuated by the unknown circumstances in which it arrived in Lichfield some time later. Thought to have been at Llandeilo for about two hundred years, the Gospel Book appears to have been taken to Lichfield by the late tenth century, although by what means is unknown. Perhaps, inevitably, its removal has become associated with the loss to England and Normandy of monastic treasures following the Norman settlement of Wales, even though from a chronological viewpoint this process was somewhat later.

One explanation could be that the book was a diplomatic gift, although a more likely story is that it was stolen. But it surely must be relevant that by the early eleventh century Llandeilo was in considerable decline, with its early prominence as an ecclesiastical centre by then eclipsed by Llandaff, whereas Lichfield Cathedral was the centre of a wealthy English diocese. There must certainly be a David and Goliath side to this tale.

One positive aspect, though, is that we have the opportunity to see the Gospel Book in two different places and in two very different formats. It must also be added that the authorities at Lichfield Cathedral worked together with the parish church at Llandeilo to allow the digitalisation of the book. This process was carried out using a technique pioneered by the British Library, and was the first time this had involved a manuscript not in its own possession. The American academic, Professor Bill Endres, then of the University of Kentucky, oversaw the project to considerable acclaim.[20]

My own first visit to Llandeilo also, by co-incidence, included meeting visitors from the USA. Taking part in a pilgrimage by coach to historic churches in south Wales and the west of England, this group had an hour or two in the town before continuing on to Llantwit Major the same afternoon. Astounded as they were by a history going back fifteen hundred years to the Age of the Saints, their itinerary included Llancarfan, Brecon (*Aberhonddu*) and Hay-on-Wye (*Y Gelli Gandryll*).[21]

It was a curiously and unexpectedly international day and perhaps that's one of the benefits of the story of the Gospel Book. There may be contention surrounding it but just as the uncertainties as to its origin speak of the connectedness of the early medieval world, so in our own times it has drawn people together from across the globe.

Socket stone, St Cynwyd's Church, Llangynwyd and the Margam Stones Museum

OS: SS 858 888 | OS: SS 802 863

Walking on pilgrimage across south Wales, I was interested to come across the socket stone to be found at the parish church in Llangynwyd. The stone is attached by a metal bracket to the north wall of the porch.

I was intrigued to see this because the only previous time I had seen a socket stone of this type was at Old Kirk Braddan near Douglas (*Doolish*) on the Isle of Man. There, two examples are on display in the church, among a collection of several crosses and incised stones dating from about 900 to the thirteenth century.

Such stones are very difficult to date because, unlike the crosses and slabs they were used to support, they do not have any inscriptions or decorative work on them, although it can be seen that use has been made of the south Wales stone for much later graffiti, whereas one of the examples at Braddan has a small cross incised on it, although there is no indication of the date of this. As a result, it has to be assumed that socket stones belong in the same context as the early medieval crosses and slabs among which, as at Braddan, they find themselves today.

Such stones would have served rather like a collar. With their long side horizontal to the ground, they would have been placed in a shallow pit (and possibly also with other socket stones beneath them to provide further support) to hold up, in a vertical position, the much more important cross or slab to which they were only an adjunct.[22]

Interestingly, the Isle of Man is also home to a particularly stunning early medieval cross in the churchyard at Lonan Old Church (*Kirk Lonan*). There, not only is the cross thought to be in its original position but its socket stone is still clearly visible.

Meanwhile, back in south Wales, who knows what splendid artefact the humble stone at Llangynwyd may have supported?

However, perhaps we can have some idea of this from the fabulous Margam Stones Museum.[23] This is a place that is comparable with what can seem to be much more prestigious venues, such as the Abbey Museum on Iona, but is situated just a few miles from Llangynwyd along the course of an old drove road.

With the collection being originally brought together in the nineteenth century by the Talbot family, then owners of the Margam Estate, its particular glory is twelve sculptured crosses and cross slabs dating from about 900 to 1100. All coming from Margam itself, or what is now Port Talbot and the hill farms nearby, these monuments indicate that there must have been a considerable religious community, with a school of sculpture, in or near Margam that preceded its foundation as a Cistercian abbey in the twelfth century.

Today, this area can seem to be defined by the huge steelworks and the M4 motorway, but the surviving early medieval crosses place Margam firmly within a rich heritage of stone sculpture in south Wales. And although it's not always obvious what purpose these artefacts served – whether as memorials to individuals, a focus for more general burials, as waymarkers or serving the purpose of sanctifying a space or delineating territory – their impact today can feel all the more vivid considering the nature of the locality as we now experience it.

As regards socket stones, one of the crosses in the collection, the cross of Grutne, has a slight tenon at its base that would have slotted into such a device, although this would only work if the tenon was considerably larger than what we see today. However, the cross of Conbelin,[24] which makes a splendid focal point in the building, is supported by a large cuboid base, complete with a hunting scene and geometrical patterns. This is clearly very different to the modest stone as found at Llangynwyd, and still to be seen in situ at Lonan, and perhaps has more in common, at least in a practical sense, with the pedestal-type socket stones of later medieval churchyard crosses. These are discussed in the next chapter.

Meanwhile, a possible intermediate style between the quite roughly made socket stone at Llangynwyd and later examples might perhaps be seen in the stone to be found in the churchyard at Merthyr Mawr in the Vale of Glamorgan. Dated by Cadw to the eleventh to twelfth century, this is larger than what can be seen at Llangynwyd and the rectangular cavity to hold the cross is more precisely formed. Believed to have come from the area of sand dunes known as Merthyr Mawr Warren, and to have been found with fragments of a cross,[25] the socket stone is situated near the parking area.

CHAPTER 5

A new order?

SOMETHING THAT I never tire of seeing as I make my way on my pilgrimages are the later medieval crosses which are so frequently found in churchyards in Wales and England. There they remain for the contemporary visitor or pilgrim to discover.

Like the Celtic crosses such as can be seen at Margam, they probably owe their distant origins to the wooden crosses carried as standards by the earliest church-planters, although any relationship between these three phases remains unclear. What we do know, though, is that later medieval churchyard crosses often suffered deliberate, albeit partial, destruction following on from the Reformation, as well as neglect in more recent centuries. What can be seen today can vary from little more than a heap of stones to some still very impressive structures that have survived thanks to local circumstances. This is certainly the case as regards the cross at Tremeirchion in north Wales, discussion of which forms the first section of this chapter.

Something else which can be viewed, whether the church building is open or not, is the remarkable Romanesque doorway at Llanbadarn Fawr near Llandrindod Wells. Associated with the earliest phase of building in stone in Wales (after the long-departed Romans), this intriguing feature forms part of what is now a largely Victorian building.

Also 'open all hours' are the remains of St Mary's Abbey on the island of Bardsey (*Yyns Enlli*), although you will need to make a boat trip from the mainland to get there.

However, what this ruined abbey, Romanesque doorway and churchyard cross also all have in common is their association with the later medieval period in Wales after the Normans – having rapidly seized power in England following William the Conqueror's victory at Hastings – moved on into Wales from about 1080. With the nation still divided into fractious small kingdoms, the Norman kings used a system of Marcher Lordships by which high-ranking supporters, whose family roots were in Normandy, were given large swathes of land not only along the border with England but also extending into Pembrokeshire and north-east Wales. The object of this policy was to devolve power and authority to these men to enable them to resist opposition from the Welsh and also to give them opportunities to gain further territory within Wales for themselves and their dynasties.

This resulted in a very piecemeal, and frequently changing, situation as regards the holding of land and the concomitant wielding of power, although the general direction was one of increasing subjection to the Normans. By the late thirteenth century Edward I of England, in his conquest of Wales, furthered this process of acquisition. This then led to a situation whereby some territory was held directly by the English monarch, while a substantial area of Wales remained in the control of the Marcher Lords who, at least in theory, were subject to him. This state of affairs continued until the time of the Tudors when two Acts of Parliament, in the reign of Henry VIII (reigned 1509–1547), annexed Wales to England.

St Mary's Abbey, Bardsey Island

OS: SH 120 223

Bardsey is well known in Wales and beyond as a place of great beauty and considerable isolation, continuing to draw people who seek a peaceful atmosphere and a gentler pace of life, even if only for a few hours. Today, it's the property of the Bardsey

Island Trust and a National Nature Reserve and Site of Special Scientific Interest, but it's the island's place in the religious history of Wales that has really set it apart.

With the founding of a simple monastery perhaps as early as the sixth century, and its reputation as the burial place of 20,000 saints, including the notable St Deiniol and St Dyfrig,[1] Bardsey soon became one of the great pilgrimage centres of Wales.

Situated about two miles across the treacherous Bardsey Sound (*Swnt Enlli*), the very considerable number of pilgrims wanting to reach the island has shaped not only the history but also the geography of this area of north Wales. Coming down the Llŷn peninsula, the ancient network of roads and tracks clearly leads to Bardsey at its very tip. Although now a popular holiday destination, the pattern of the roads on the peninsula points to a past where the objective of most travellers was the 'island in the currents' two miles out in the Irish Sea.

Although as a child I had often been one of the many tourists in this area, it was only when I was making my way around Wales on my very first pilgrimage that I finally got to go to Bardsey, this being the culmination of two weeks' walking from near Holywell (*Treffynnon*) in Flintshire (*Sir y Fflint*) on the North Wales Pilgrim's Way. In doing this, I was very fortunate to have been 'adopted' by a group of pilgrims who had pioneered this route under the leadership of Chris Potter, a former Archdeacon of the Diocese of St Asaph (*Esgobaeth Llanelwy*) and Dean of the cathedral. Having walked the famous *Camino* to Santiago de Compostela with his wife, Jenny, they had returned to north Wales determined to set up something similar in their own area, with its particularly rich Christian heritage.[2]

When I walked with the group that year, the project was already well-advanced and much progress had been made. There were just some final details to check, among which was ensuring that the distinctive waymarkers on fence posts were facing the right direction and so on.

It was a great privilege to walk with this enterprising band of pilgrims for that fortnight, and I remain very grateful for all their help. Just one aspect of this was that they had booked a dozen places on the boat to Bardsey for when they all arrived at Aberdaron, the little ferry embarking from the slipway at Porth Meudwy a mile or so from the main village. With many campsites, holiday homes and hotels in the locality, it was essential to book tickets in advance for the day trip to the island, but with more than twelve of us in the group, I was kindly allowed one of the places available. As most of these north Wales pilgrims had previously been over to the island, I was made a priority for a ticket as I had never been there before. I'm not sure I would have managed to organise this for myself, so their kindness and forward planning meant a great deal to me.

Following a rather rough crossing with the wind being so strong that the boat was close to being cancelled due to bad weather, we finally arrived. Encouraged by having seen my first puffin as we made our way across the sound, it was a considerable relief to be on dry ground with several hours ahead of me to explore just a little of what the island has to offer.

However, one of the things that especially intrigued me that day was the story of Bardsey's St Mary's Abbey, of which just one tower remains in the corner of a graveyard. Making my way to the tiny settlement where the ruins can be seen, it was extraordinary to think that, until the Dissolution of the Monasteries in the reign of Henry VIII, this small island had been home to an Augustinian religious house.

Known as Canons Regular, these men followed a rule based on the teachings of St Augustine of Hippo (354–430). Although they lived in community, their vows allowed them to travel to the mainland where they acted as clergy for local parishes.

These seem to have included the village of Llanengan, about ten miles away, near Abersoch. There, in the parish church of St Engan, a sturdy oak chest and two very striking sets of choir stalls can be seen, these probably being brought over from Bardsey at the time of the Dissolution.[3]

However, the canons must have had other parishes who looked to them for support, and spent perhaps months at a time on the mainland where they would have officiated at Mass, heard confessions, and conducted baptisms and funerals. In doing so, they were part of a system of pastoral care that was increasingly the model across Western Europe, where parishes were becoming formalised and provision for the spiritual life of a growing population was becoming more uniform.

How to balance these considerations, with a concern for the appropriate support of the clergy, had led to the emergence of the Augustinian Canons Regular in Italy in the eleventh century. With other groupings of canons also appearing at this time, the intention was to ensure that correct discipline was maintained among these men as they went about their work among the ordinary people.

Different from cloistered monks, who took a vow of stability and who were generally not priests, Canons Regular were free from the constraint of staying within the abbey and its lands, allowing them to travel to parishes in their care. However, this would clearly lead to worldly temptations, hence the commitment to living in a community when not involved in pastoral work.

At a time when the role of parish priest was just beginning to emerge, the canons were perhaps something of a hybrid between that function and that of a monk. In practice, though, we have little idea how this really worked from the point of view of either the men themselves or the parishioners whom they ministered to. We also don't know to what extent they were local people or whether they were drafted in from other areas and even from mainland Europe.[4]

But what is especially interesting about the Augustinian house at St Mary's Abbey is how far it was a continuum of the early medieval monastery on the island, and by what means the one had evolved into the other. That this happened seems almost certain, as there is no evidence for a re-founding of the abbey or for an end to the previous Celtic foundation.[5] Along with other houses of Canons Regular in north Wales, it would appear that the Augustinian rule was gradually adopted over a century or so.

Travelling in this area in 1188, Gerald of Wales describes the monks on Bardsey as *Céli Dé*,[6] a term associated with Irish spirituality and the reinvigoration of early monasticism. There is no mention or hint from him of what would become St Mary's Abbey and an Augustinian house. Yet, by 1212, canons from Bardsey were at the Augustinian abbey at Haughmond[7], near Shrewsbury, to witness a charter. Therefore, it would appear that somewhere between these two occasions St Mary's Abbey became part of what was then a loose confederation of similar houses to be found not only in north Wales but also elsewhere in the British Isles, and more widely in Western Europe. In this, the island of Bardsey, with its community of Canons Regular, was drawn into contemporary changes in the pastoral care of the laity that reached far beyond Wales.

However, this was a time of considerable development for all those involved in the professed religious life. For although monasticism had been a feature of Christianity since the third century, those living under monastic vows had generally followed the example of a local abbot and his rule, this being far removed from the often large and centralised religious orders that would characterise the later medieval period.

In this, Wales was the same as elsewhere, with her simple early monasteries having their counterparts in the rest of the British Isles and further afield. But, like everywhere else, these earlier foundations, as on Bardsey, were now unlikely to survive in their original form. Some seem to have disbanded or been discontinued, but others became drawn into the more formal communities that were being established. Thus, there seems to have been a pattern whereby some of the traditional Celtic *clasau*,[8] which had developed over centuries to provide for congregations served by smaller subsidiary churches, evolved to become houses of Canons Regular. With clearly similar aims, becoming an Augustinian community was perhaps a natural progression in an increasingly integrated Europe.[9] In this way, St Mary's Abbey would have taken its place not only among other houses of the same order but also the wider landscape of Benedictine, Cistercian and other religious communities.

And although it's perhaps easy to see these changes as flowing inevitably from the growing power of the Normans in Wales, the trend towards a greater uniformity in religious life can be seen in neighbouring England even before the Norman Conquest. And while the comments made by Gerald of Wales suggest the process of change was slow, there does seem to be a certain inevitability about it as Europe moved into the what is sometimes referred to, retrospectively of course, as the High Middle Ages.

As with all religious houses across Wales and England, it was another political upheaval in the form of the Dissolution of the Monasteries that marked the end of St Mary's Abbey on Bardsey. The canons would have received modest pensions, and the assets of the Abbey removed and sold. With the parish church at Llanengan known to have been rebuilt in the 1530s, it would seem to be at this point that the oak chest and choir stalls were taken over to the mainland.

The Romanesque tympanum, St Padarn's Church, Llanbadarn Fawr, Powys

OS: SO 087 643

There is a moral to be learned from visiting St Padarn's Church, just a few miles to the north-east of Llandrindod

Wells: that is to never underestimate what may appear to be yet another rather dull Victorian restoration or rebuild of an earlier medieval church.

Approaching from the east and having just come across the very quiet area of Radnor Forest (*Fforest Glud*), I was enjoying being back in Wales as I walked from Lichfield to Llandeilo. However, I remember the moment of temptation when I considered not crossing the quite busy main road to get to St Padarn's Church on the other side. After all, what interest could such a place hold and weren't such churches, with their suburban demeanour, often locked?

But, of course, this is not the attitude of the determined pilgrim, and reminding myself of its Celtic dedication I soon relented, crossed the road and found this welcoming church with its open door.

However, it was the surround to that unlocked door which immediately caught my attention: an extraordinary Romanesque tympanum and carved pillars with fantastical designs. Going inside, a useful booklet[10] and other information available at the site provided an introduction to understanding these remarkable features on the south side of the church, which are placed within a relatively modern porch.

The tympanum, that is the semi-circular panel above the door, is carved with a simple tree coming out of the top of a lion or cat's head. On each side of the tree, a lion with a long tail appears to eat its leaves, the animal on the right perhaps more obviously leonine than the one to the left, which has a star-type symbol close to its paws. In both examples, their long tails come from between their hind legs up to almost level with their heads.

On the capitals of the small pillars on each side of the door, other carvings are to be found with human heads, dragons, and two small full-length figures. Meanwhile, the arch above the tympanum has repeated rows of a chevron design with another geometric pattern on the lintel. In addition, three other old stones are set within the porch, these being a head with two faces, a possible Sheela Na Gig[11] and a Roman stone with a Latin inscription.[12]

That these features have survived at all seems close to miraculous, remnants as they are of the earlier medieval church which stood here until the rebuilding of the church in 1878–79 by the well-known architect Stephen W. Williams. As a small doorway on the south side and windows in the east wall also retain their medieval form and material, it would seem that Williams did not entirely dismiss the architectural value of St Padarn's as he found it. However, he has to be included in the generally maligned group of nineteenth-century architects who are seen as responsible for the destruction or unsympathetic restoration of medieval churches not only in Wales but also in England and across the British Isles.

Unfortunately, we have only scant details about the condition of St Padarn's before its rebuilding; only a paper, *Notes upon some Radnorshire churches*, written by Williams in 1874, and including a drawing of the Romanesque doorway as then attached to the medieval stonework – gives any indication of the church at that time. Of course, it is possible that the building was much decayed, with other Romanesque work seeming to have been lost to later architectural styles long before the nineteenth century. In short, we can't blame Williams for everything and we certainly need to be thankful for what can still be seen at the church today.

This itself raises various important points, the most fundamental of which is that of the use of stone in the construction of churches across Wales, with the remains of the Romanesque church almost certainly being from the earliest such building on the site. Secondly, there is then is the issue of patronage, that is who was responsible for this development and what were the stylistic influences on them? And underlying everything, there is the debate about whether those influences were coming from within Wales, or from

England and its relatively new masters, or even from further afield.

It has been shown that Wales enjoyed a considerable flowering of Romanesque ecclesiastical architecture. And while some of this – such as the rebuilding of Llandaff Cathedral under Bishop Urban in the 1120s – is firmly rooted in the Norman settlement of Wales, other examples, such as the only other surviving Romanesque tympanum, at Penmon Priory (*Priordy a Chroes Penmon*) on Anglesey, may speak of a truly Welsh interpretation of this European-wide style.

To this end, the case has also been made that the figures on the capital of the left-hand pillar at Llanbadarn Fawr are taken from an episode in the *Life of St Padarn*,[13] written at the larger church of the same name in Ceredigion in about 1100. With this west Wales church then coming under the unwelcome authority of the Norman abbey of St Peter's in Gloucester, if the figures really are Padarn and his opponent, the tyrant Arthur, then Welsh influence on the Romanesque church at Llanbadarn Fawr would seem to be significant.[14]

However, overall, the opinion is that the designs on the tympanum itself, and of the doorway as a whole, are derived from similar Norman work in England. This is because 'tree of life' tympana, with accompanying animals, are found scattered across the midlands and south of the country.[15] There is also the considerable influence of the Herefordshire and Dymock schools of Romanesque architecture on the wider area of the Marches, with the church here at Llanbadarn Fawr considered to be an outlier of this group. As to timing, the Romanesque doorway is thought to date from the mid-twelfth century when the more sophisticated examples, such as at Kilpeck and Shobdon, not far away in England, were beginning to be imitated by less highly skilled craftsmen.

In addition, the proximity of a Norman motte or castle mound only about a mile away at Old Castle could be an indicator that the Mortimer dynasty of Marcher Lords, the builders of the fortification at this point close to the River Ithon (*Afon Leithon*), may have been the patrons of the church at this phase in its building. If this is the case, Llanbadarn Fawr would be one of many churches in the borderlands of Wales and England where Romanesque architecture was fostered by a Norman elite.

The more general history of St Padarn's is also of interest. Although, as mentioned previously, it is one of three dedications to Padarn in this area, it is thought that the church was the principal one in the ancient lordship of Maelienydd, situated between the Severn and the Wye. Making a visit as Archdeacon of Brecon in 1176, Gerald of Wales recorded that there were 'six or seven clerks, who after the Welsh fashion shared the church between them', which strongly suggests that the church was a *clas*, as does the fact that it was seen as a suitable location for the gathering or synod Gerald hoped to convene.

However, the archdeacon had not heeded warnings from local clergy that he was not welcome, and should send a representative rather than attend in person. The unfortunate Gerald was then kidnapped and held against his will in the church until the local prince, Cadwallon ap Madoc, together his wife Eva, secured his release.

It's fascinating to reflect that the Romanesque tympanum is likely to have been seen by Gerald when it was still quite new, as he was bustled into the building by his captors that day!

The churchyard cross, Tremeirchion

OS: SJ 083 731

When walking in Wales, apart from churches themselves, perhaps the most frequently seen Christian symbol and religious structure would be the many crosses that are found across the country. A common feature in Anglican churchyards, including many examples in England, these are part of a wider landscape of stone crosses ranging from early medieval high crosses to market crosses of the later Middle Ages and the very widespread war memorials of the twentieth century. However, my focus here is on the crosses dating from the twelfth century to the sixteenth century, found within churchyards and, in particular, the story of the exceptional example to be found at Tremeirchion, near St Asaph (*Llanelwy*).

The medieval churches of Wales are frequently accompanied by the remains of such a cross, typically on the south side of the church and not far from what is usually the main door into the building. Mounted on a roughly square stepped base, a large cuboid socket stone is often still in place to support a tapering vertical shaft which, just occasionally, is still capped with the original head. Variously called a tabernacle, lantern or rood, this uppermost section typically includes a crucifixion scene, with the Virgin and Child depicted on the opposite face.

But whereas most churchyard crosses consist of a base, socket stone and shaft (with often considerable restoration over the centuries being evident) but no head to be seen, the opposite is the case at Tremeirchion. Here, in this north Wales village, the lovely rood is now back in the churchyard under an ancient yew tree, albeit on a modern base and shaft erected in 2005. Meanwhile, closer to the door of the church and approximately where the cross would have stood in medieval times, what is thought to be the original shaft (although apparently inverted), has served as the base for a sundial since the eighteenth century.

With the story of the Tremeirchion cross being both typical and yet very different to what has happened to the many other examples over the years, the result is the unusual but ultimately satisfying circumstances that we find it in today.

As with other medieval churchyard crosses, the one at Tremeirchion would have stood as a sign of the sanctification of burials that took place around it. With graves generally being unmarked in medieval times, the presence of the cross would have declared Christian belief in the forgiveness of sin brought about by Christ's death, and of the hope of eternal life and resurrection. The cross would also have been a station in the processions, notably on Palm Sunday and the local saint's day (or here at Tremeirchion on the feast of Corpus Christi) which were part of the religious customs of the time.

In addition, with the Mass being the focus of worship within the church building, on the rare occasions when a sermon was preached this generally would have taken place outside at the cross afterwards, resulting in these structures sometimes being referred to as 'preaching crosses'. In the case of the Tremeirchion cross, it would also seem that it was seen as a source of healing, with people visiting it on pilgrimage. Its curative powers were described in a poem written in about 1500 by Welsh bard Gruffydd ab Ieuan ab Llewelyn Fychan of nearby Llanerch.[16]

However, the momentous religious changes brought about at the Reformation in the sixteenth century, and the puritan zeal that often followed, were not kind to churchyard crosses. With the new Protestantism favouring the primacy of the Bible and the exposition of God's Word, preaching became a more frequent element in Sunday worship, with pews increasingly provided from the later years of Elizabeth I. Thus, with the congregation sitting inside, the churchyard cross no longer functioned as a place for the priest to deliver a sermon. Meanwhile, the observance of church feasts and saints' days, which were a considerable part of the now discontinued Catholic liturgy, did not feature so prominently in worship as authorised by the newly established Anglican Church.

But it was the inclusion of religious images, and even the image of the cross itself, that was probably the death knell for churchyard crosses, with Parliament in the 1640s ordering their destruction over a certain height.[17] It would seem to be at this time that they were often finally destroyed, with just the base and perhaps the lower section of the shaft left in place, resulting in what is so often still to be seen in churchyards across Wales.

But it appears that, as with many items associated with the earlier Catholic worship in medieval churches, what happened in these turbulent centuries depended very much on local sentiment and the opinions and actions of churchwardens and others. With some evidence that the ornate uppermost sections of these structures were not necessarily done away with, this appears to have been the course of events at Tremeirchion. Travelling in north Wales in 1770, the traveller and antiquarian Thomas Pennant (1726–1798) recorded that, although the lower section of the cross had been destroyed, 'the carved capital is still to be seen, in a building adjoining the churchyard'.[18] This is believed to be from where it was taken in about 1862 when it was purchased for £5 by Mr J.Y. Hynde of Rhyl, with the money raised being used to purchase lamps for the church. He then presented it to the new College of St Beuno a mile or so from Tremeirchion.

Then a recently-established Jesuit seminary for the training of Roman Catholic priests, the head of the cross was erected on a new plinth and shaft outside the college where it stayed until the millennium year, when it was generously returned by the college to the Anglican parish church. With a modern base and shaft placed close to a yew tree, and believed to be where Pennant's 'building adjoining the churchyard' stood, the head of the cross has now been on public view since 2005. With perhaps two hundred years of its existence spent in its shelter in the churchyard and also careful guardianship at St Beuno's, its state of preservation is very good and the cross makes a rather splendid sight for visitors and local people alike.

However, another facet to this story is that the Victorian poet Gerard Manley Hopkins was a seminarian at St Beuno's College in the time when the Tremeirchion cross was situated there. And although Hopkins' writings make no mention of it, with the considerable influence of Wales and Welsh poetry on his work there's a rather happy connection between the poet and the remarkable story of the cross.[19] With Hopkins converting to Catholicism amidst a fractured nineteenth-century religious landscape, the cross has survived into our own times to be a symbol of a shared Christian heritage.

Seeing the Tremeirchion churchyard cross for the first time when I was walking with the north Wales pilgrims, and being made aware of the role of St Beuno's College (now a Residential Retreat Centre[20]) in its preservation, two things of great interest to me were combined. With a love for Hopkins' poetry fostered when I was a schoolgirl in south Wales, and with the continued interest I feel when I see yet another churchyard cross, Tremeirchion seemed very special that day and, indeed, remains so.

CHAPTER 6

Pilgrimage in Wales

As a TWENTY-FIRST century pilgrim, I am especially interested to see things that relate to pilgrimage in its heyday in the later Middle Ages, when visiting the shrines of saints was at its most popular.

In earlier centuries, travelling a long distance, perhaps even to Jerusalem or Rome, was almost exclusively the preserve of churchmen, the wealthy and the powerful. Ordinary folk would simply not have had the means to travel or would have been content to visit simple shrines to local saints.

However, in the Norman period and up until the Reformation, making a pilgrimage became much more commonplace, often with the object of praying for healing or expressing penitence. People also seem to have started going longer distances to the great shrines such as at St Davids (*Tyddewi*) or to St Winefride's Well at Holywell. Pilgrims from Wales would also have made their way to places such as Canterbury and Walsingham or the Holy Rood of Chester.

With larger numbers of pilgrims travelling, what we would call an infrastructure came into being with wayside crosses marking routes, subsidiary chapels along the way, and also places to lodge and eat. But these early travellers still faced considerable dangers and generally walked or rode in groups for safety. They also wore distinctive dress to mark them out as legitimate wayfarers, and not mere vagabonds who would be sent back to their home parish.

Sadly, perhaps, the popularity of pilgrimage was brought to an end at the Reformation, when the new theology of

Protestantism opposed not only the veneration of saints but also their role as intercessors for the living. As a result, the authorities often destroyed shrines, leaving little or no trace of these substantial structures. Meanwhile, the Dissolution of the Monasteries had the effect of removing the network of pilgrim hospices, as these were generally provided by religious houses.

However, in spite of this onslaught, at least at Holywell it seems that people continued to make pilgrimages, albeit in smaller numbers. Perhaps because of the draw of such a notable natural phenomenon, St Winefride's Well appears to have continued to receive pilgrims throughout the centuries when the earlier beliefs and practices were proscribed.[1]

Moreover, in our own times, a few medieval shrines have been rebuilt, notably that of St Melangell[2] at her church in the Berwyn mountains of north Wales. Here, some of the long-discarded stone from the original Romanesque structure was recovered from the churchyard and has been used to restore the shrine which now draws considerable numbers of modern-day pilgrims.

The Hospital of St Mary the Virgin, St Thomas the Martyr and Edward the King, Llawhaden

OS: SN 075 174

I have yet to find a place in Wales that doesn't claim to be or have been on a pilgrim route to St Davids. Of course, this is an exaggeration, but the attraction of this tiny cathedral city to long-gone and also contemporary pilgrims seems unsurpassed, certainly within Wales. Situated within an area of stunning natural beauty and taking pride of place in Britain's only coastal national park,[3] St Davids is also surrounded by an extraordinary religious landscape at least in part formed by its popularity as a place of pilgrimage in the Middle Ages.

For medieval pilgrims, the object of their frequently long

journeys was the shrine of St David where they would have uttered their prayers close to the reliquary believed to contain his remains. (In 1081 their numbers even included William the Conqueror.) Thus, petitions for healing and forgiveness would have joined the intercessions of the greatest saint of Wales. For such was the power of David's cult, and a cynic might say that this was carefully nurtured in the Norman period, that the twelfth-century pope, Callixtus II, declared that two pilgrimages to St Davids would equal one to the great holy city of Rome, whereas three would be commensurate with going on pilgrimage to Jerusalem.

With so many pilgrims wanting go to St Davids, routes by both land and sea not only from Wales and England but also further afield from Ireland and Brittany began to be established.

As I walked around Wales on my first pilgrimage, I too joined the many thousands that St Davids continues to attract.[4] In doing so, my route would have been similar to that of medieval pilgrims journeying from north Wales and the north of England, taking me through places such as Nevern (*Nanhyfer*) in Pembrokeshire. Here, pilgrims seem to have knelt in prayer and added their own mark to a cross incised on a rocky outcrop as they made their way down a lane near the ancient church of St Brynach.[5]

However, it was on my onward journey across south Wales that I came across the remains of the Hospital at Llawhaden (*Llanhuadain*). This would have been along the pilgrim route for those coming from south Wales and the English Midlands. With such a volume of travellers from these areas, various different itineraries seem to have evolved; another road took a more southerly route.

With both the Welsh and English words derived from the Latin *hospitium*, what can be seen at Llawhaden is a hospital (*ysbyty*) in the original sense of the word, that is, a place for the care of those in various sorts of need. This would have included not only pilgrims but also the infirm and the destitute, with what can be seen of the former hospital at Llawhaden being one of the most complete examples of such structures in the British Isles.

It was also just one of several similar institutions in what is now Pembrokeshire that would have offered lodging, food and medical care. Other places included St Mary's Hospice at nearby Spittal (where the name of the village is also derived from *hospitium*) and Whitewell Hospital in St Davids itself.[6]

However, it's uncertain just what function the building as seen today served. Traditionally, it had been thought to be a chapel because it contains a *piscina*, that is the stone basin used for the washing of Communion vessels, but it could have been a dormitory, refectory or infirmary. Now in the care of Cadw, it can't be entered but only viewed from the exterior, where information is available. It's also now known to have been part of a bigger complex of buildings of which it seems to have been the last to be constructed. Established by Bishop Bec in 1287, the hospitality it provided was supervised by a prior and a small group of monastic brothers. As with all foundations of this sort, it ceased to function in the late 1530s as a consequence of the Dissolution of the Monasteries in Wales and England by Thomas Cromwell (*c*.1485–1540), the chief minister of Henry VIII.

The Hospital at Llawhaden was also part of the wider reach of Norman power in west Wales in the Middle Ages. Owned by the bishops of St Davids on whose extensive lands it was placed, their status as Marcher Lords gave them authority to dispense justice and raise armies as agents of the kings of England. On this basis the area around Llawhaden, as well as the pre-Norman cantref of Dewisland surrounding St Davids itself, was held in a similar way to the Marcher lands of south Wales and the border country to the east. The bishops also held the nearby castle,[7] which acted as their administrative centre. Their activities included the settlement of Llawhaden as a borough, with the medieval burgage plots still evident in the layout of the village today.

Llawhaden's importance to the Normans also persists in its place on the English side of the Landsker line which continues to mark the linguistic division of Pembrokeshire into Welsh- and English-speaking areas.

In addition, the Hospital's dedication to St Mary the Virgin, St Thomas the Martyr, and Edward the King is an indicator of its status as a Norman institution. Dedications to St Mary in Wales nearly always relate to Norman settlement and the accompanying establishment of new churches and religious houses. To this day they are more prevalent in areas that were held as Marcher lordships. St Thomas the Martyr is also very much a Norman saint, with Thomas Becket's dispute with Henry II leading to his murder in 1170 and then to his canonisation by the pope soon afterwards. The Norman kings also saw themselves as the rightful successors to Edward the Confessor, whose death in 1066 led to various claims to the throne of England, with William the Conqueror being the eventual victor.

Coming across the Hospital at Llawhaden was a timely reminder to me of my own practical needs as pilgrim. As with my medieval predecessors, I also needed food and shelter. That June day I had approached from Spittal, where I had been kindly welcomed at a very quiet campsite where I appeared to be the only person staying. No sooner had I put down my backpack and begun to pitch my tent, a much-appreciated mug of tea and plate of biscuits had been brought out to me!

The Pilgrim Cross at Bwlch y Groes

OS: SH 914 229

The wooden cross at Bwlch y Groes (*Pass of the Cross*) shows something of the significance of this now very quiet place to medieval pilgrims as they made their way across Wales from

Holywell in north-east Wales to St Davids in the south-west. With the present cross put in position on Holy Cross Day (14 September) 1989 to mark a pilgrimage organised by the Diocese of Bangor (*Esgobaeth Bangor*), it is successor to a medieval one in the same position and can be found just below the highest point on this mountain pass, near to a junction where another minor road goes off to the east towards the reservoir at Lake Vyrnwy (*Llyn Efyrnwy*).

Not that anyone would be likely to miss this landmark at such a lonely spot in the southern reaches of the Eryri National Park (*Parc Cenedlaethol Eryri*). My abiding memory of being there is one of almost total silence and of the bleak magnificence of the landscape.[8] Apart from a very occasional car passing me and, once or twice, the call of a buzzard, I heard nothing for the hour or so it took me to walk up from Llanymawddwy as I made my way across Wales to Holyhead (*Caergybi*) and on to Ireland.

However, it has not always been so, with the information board at the highest point of the pass[9] describing how the road was used by the Austin Motor Company in the 1920s and 1930s to test drive new vehicles. Bwlch y Groes was also important in the development of motorcycle engines, with the steep climbs in both directions providing a suitable challenge in assessing the endurance of those machines.

Of course, medieval pilgrims did not have to concern themselves with fast cars and speeding motor bikes, but their route would still have been busy by the standards of the time as the mountain pass was then on the main road from north to south Wales. For although the modern main road takes a longer way round through Dolgellau to the west, the more direct route over Bwlch y Groes was the thoroughfare until the age of the internal combustion engine.

It was in this context that what seems to us a minor mountain road was included in the modern world's first ever road atlas, when John Ogilby published his *Britannia* in 1685.

Covering seventy-three major roads across Wales and England, Ogilby's surveying and mapping of the 156-mile route between Holywell and St Davids was just part of this pioneering project, which included 7,500 miles of what were then important postal routes.

The road maps in Ogilby's enormous book used a scale of one inch to a mile, and took the form of six strips working from left to right across each page in a scrolling effect, rather like a modern sat-nav. A compass rose indicated each change of direction, with a set of symbols indicating essential landmarks to the traveller's right or left. However, any traveller would have needed to be of the armchair kind as the book was so large and heavy, although later revisions were smaller and more practical.[10]

It can be easy to forget that Ogilby's work paved the way, almost literally, for modern road maps. Earlier seventeenth-century cartographers, such as John Speed and Gerard Mercator, did not include roads on their maps at all. Ogilby also consistently used the mile of 1,760 yards, as established by statute of 1593, even though there were still many variations in use in Wales and England at this time.

The Shrine of St Winefride, Shrewsbury Abbey

OS: SJ 498 125

I had the opportunity to visit the shrine of St Winefride at Shrewsbury Abbey as I walked south down the English side of the border with Wales on my return from the Isle of Man. What particularly intrigued me was that Winefride, so closely associated with north Wales, had gone on to achieve a wider fame and veneration once her relics had been translated to Shrewsbury Abbey in the Norman period. Now, what has survived of Winefride's medieval shrine can be seen reconstructed rather like an altar in the north aisle of the abbey, where it makes a lovely reminder of the importance of such features in the later Middle Ages. With several small vases of fresh flowers placed on it and a modern icon of the saint to one side, a fine, arcaded section of the shrine with low relief sculptures of Winifred, Beuno, and John the Baptist has been placed in a position similar to a reredos.

What can be seen today at the abbey probably dates from a rebuilding of her shrine in the fourteenth century, being recovered from a local garden relatively recently and known to have previously been used as building stone for a bridge. However, this has just been part of Winefride's long and interesting journey from her original home in seventh-century Flintshire to contemporary Shrewsbury, with fresh evidence for her cult coming to light as recently as the 1990s.

In the past the historicity of Winefride's early life in what is now the Holywell area of north Wales has often been doubted, with no mention of her in Welsh or English sources before the twelfth century. With her name in Welsh, Gwenffrewi, possibly derived from words describing the gushing spring known as St Winefride's Well, the story of her death by decapitation at the hands of an unwelcome suitor and her subsequent healing through the intervention of her uncle, the saintly Beuno, clearly lends itself to being considered a mere legend. Moreover, the main source of information about Winefride's life is the twelfth-century *Vita* by Robert of Shrewsbury, then prior of Shrewsbury Abbey and the person through whose efforts her relics were acquired. Being written soon after these were brought to the abbey, Robert of Shrewsbury had an obvious vested interest in promoting Winefride's sanctity at a time when his community needed some good publicity concerning its valuable new assets.

Robert of Shrewsbury also wrote an additional account of the circumstances surrounding his acquisition of the relics from the shrine at Gwytherin, now in Denbighshire, where Winefride spent the later part of her life. Although doubtless written in all seriousness at the time, this document contains several episodes that seem almost comic to us today. He describes how, following a miraculous healing after two of the brothers go to 'the fountain of St Wenefreda' to say Mass, he and a few others set off for Gwytherin. Once there, although he claims to have gained the support of the Bishop of Bangor for his cause, some of the local people remain unconvinced and one even has to be bribed before Robert and his party can take what they want and get back to Shrewsbury. Finally successful, as they approach the abbey on their return journey, another miracle occurs to demonstrate the righteousness of their actions.

Robert of Shrewsbury also draws attention to the pressure the religious house had been under because of its previous lack of relics with which to attract pilgrims. Writing about the monks of the community, Robert observes that, 'having very much lamented among themselves, that they were very deficient in reliques of saints, they mainly applied their minds to obtain them', revealing a very real need to augment the abbey's income.[11]

Modern scholarship has also corroborated the prior's concerns, demonstrating the considerable economic pressure he was under at the time as other religious houses not only had more success in drawing in pilgrims but also in exploiting such assets as bridges over the Severn. In addition, it is also now thought that Robert of Shrewsbury may have been an antecedent of the Pennant family of north-east Wales, and that his interest in Winefride's relics may reflect his own background and knowledge of the area.

More recent history has also served to justify his regard for Winefride's sanctity and her status as a real person rather than just a legendary figure. It has also drawn attention to Gwytherin as the centre of Winefride's cult from the early Middle Ages and until her relics were translated to Shrewsbury.

Visiting Gwytherin in the late seventeenth century, the antiquarian Edward Lhuyd (1660–1709) made a sketch of a reliquary then held at the parish church, which is believed to have been on the same site as the monastery to which Winefride retired as a nun. Later drawings made from his work show a wooden casket with metal mounts of a design which indicates its manufacture in about the eighth century, thus providing considerable evidence for the existence of a shrine to Winefride at this location by this time. With Winefride's *Vita* stating that she became the prioress following her aunt's tenure of what may well have been a hereditary role, the survival of the reliquary into Lhuyd's time, if not beyond, is a strong indicator for the reliability of this aspect of Robert of Shrewsbury's account.

A recent twist to this story has been the discovery in 1991, at the Roman Catholic church very close to St Winefride's Well, of a very small section of the reliquary as believed to have been observed by Lhuyd. From his sketches and this fragment, the casket can be reconstructed to have been triangular in cross-section and about 40cm long and 30cm in height. Too small to contain bones, it is thought that it would have contained items placed next to her remains, thus sharing their efficacy in healing and miracles.[12]

Meanwhile, once translated to Shrewsbury Abbey, whatever Robert of Shrewsbury took from Gwytherin (clearly not the reliquary which would re-appear later) seems to have had the desired effect in attracting pilgrims and the income they provided. Probably, in 1416, these included Henry V who came after the Battle of Agincourt to walk barefoot from Shrewsbury to Holywell, perhaps as a penitent following the slaughter of defenceless French prisoners after the hostilities.[13] As Robert of Shrewsbury hoped, the veneration of Winefride went on to become more widespread in England, with her being one of only a few Welsh saints whose cults extended beyond Wales and the border area. Close to Shrewsbury, her statue can also be seen at the ruins of Haughmond Abbey just to the north of the city. There, she has joined Augustine of Hippo, St John the

Evangelist, and Thomas Becket in the premier league, so to speak. Further afield, she was the only Welsh saint chosen by Henry VII to take her place among the 107 statues of religious figures that adorned his new chapel at Westminster Abbey in the early sixteenth century. There she stands to this day, holding a palm (a symbol of pilgrimage), with a female head, a reminder of her decapitation, at her feet.

A remarkable story for a young girl who suffered such a violent assault so long ago, and one to which people as varied as twelfth-century priors, seventeenth-century antiquarians and modern historians have contributed.

CHAPTER 7

Zealots and vandals?

IN HIS PROJECT, *A Loss of Face; Iconoclasts, Zealots and Vandals*, photo-digital artist John Goto (1949–) draws attention to the huge loss of visual art in churches as a result of the religious changes of the sixteenth century which we generally summarise as the Reformation.[1] His fascinating exhibition, now available online, includes over a hundred photographs of the images of faces on rood screens that have survived in Norfolk, Suffolk and Devon, drawing attention to the ways in which these were often quite viciously defaced using various implements.

Providing a partition in medieval churches between the chancel and the nave, rood screens were made up of panels, each of which typically contained a painting of a Biblical character or saint, thus making them the target for the 'iconoclasts, zealots and vandals' who are so often associated with this era of very considerable turbulence.[2]

Goto's work doesn't include any photos of faces from rood screens in Wales (or for that matter most of England), but his observation that screens and the paintings on them were more likely to remain in place in the relatively remote areas of East Anglia and Devon almost certainly applies to Wales. Here, remarkable survivors can be found tucked away on quiet hillsides.

However, Goto's work does not deal with the image that some of the reformers found especially offensive, that is the crucifix or rood (this being the equivalent word of Anglo-Saxon derivation), which formed the focus of the structure of which the screen was only the lower part. The image of the dying Christ on the cross, so essential to medieval worshippers, was now seen as an object of idolatry rather than of worship and prayer. Thus, particularly from the early years of the reign of Elizabeth I, considerable effort was put into destroying the roods of medieval churches and the apparatus that supported them known as the loft, which we would now describe as a gallery or perhaps a mezzanine. These were positioned across the nave of the church from north to south and sometimes extending across a side aisle as well, if such existed. They were built of wood, positioned up against and just to the west of the chancel arch.

But it was not only the image of Christ which so offended some reformers, but the action of the faithful in processing past the image to pray, light candles and kiss the feet of the dying Lord. To some (and these were typically bishops especially influenced by the new theology and churchmanship), this was simply superstitious nonsense engaged in by often illiterate worshippers. The future now belonged to a reformed religious faith founded on the truth of God's word in the Bible, and its reading and proclamation.

But on a very practical level the rood had been reached by stairs, typically contained within the wall of the church and with an access point at ground level in the nave and then at the higher level of the loft. As a result, although lofts 'that were builded for idolatry' [3]were often removed from the 1560s, the staircases that served them have, in a considerable number of cases, survived into our own times.

However, the loss of many lofts and roods, together with the screens that formed the lower part of the structure, would have been just part of a complex range of religious and more general cultural changes in the years following the Reformation and continuing into the seventeenth century. These would have affected not only the appearance of churches and traditional forms of worship, but also included issues such as what to do with Roman Catholics who would not comply with the new Church of England, which at this time also included the dioceses in Wales (these had, *de facto*, been under the authority of the ecclesiastical province of Canterbury since the twelfth century). Meanwhile, this period saw the beginning of opportunities for those we often collectively describe as 'Puritans', to express their own dissatisfaction with the form of religion favoured and enforced by the state.

Thus, in this chapter my focus will be on the phenomenon of the survival of rood screen stairs in spite of the considerable structural and visual changes within churches following the Reformation, the ongoing persecution by the state of Roman Catholic clergy who persisted in ministering in Wales and England, and also the beginnings of dissent from within the Church of England on the part of those who believed that the Reformation had not gone far enough. For these purposes, the rather splendid parish church of St Matthew at Llandefalle in mid Wales, the very poignant memorial to Blessed William Davies in the Roman Catholic church at Beaumaris (*Biwmares*) on Anglesey, and a Women's Institute banner featuring the Protestant martyr John Penry in the parish church at Llangammarch Wells (*Llangamarch*), will each, respectively, serve not only as starting points for discussion but also as interesting places for the visitor or pilgrim to see for themselves.

The rood loft stairs at Llandefalle

OS: SO 108 356

In what is now thousands of miles of walking and innumerable churches visited, the parish church at Llandefalle is one of only two places where I have been able to not only climb the stairs that would have been used to reach the long-disappeared rood loft, but then also to gaze across the void in the nave where this considerable structure would have once stood. Sharing

The *Carausius* stone, with *chi-rho* symbol, at Penmachno

The *Melus Medicus* stone at Llangian

The remains of the Roman amphitheatre, Carmarthen

On the course of the Roman road on
Mynydd Bach Trecastell

Detail on the tomb of St Pompée,
Langoat

On Church Island, Anglesey

St Tysilio's Church,
Church Island

Thomas Telford's Menai
Suspension Bridge

Guriat's Cross, Kirk Maughold

The North Keeill, Kirk Maughold

St Maughold and his coracle without oars, Ramsey, Isle of Man

St Gwyddelan's Bell, Dolwyddelan

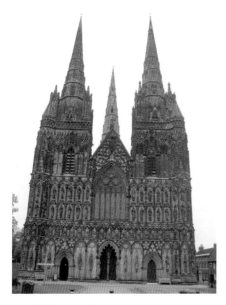

Lichfield Cathedral

Socket stone, Llangynwyd

Early medieval cross, Lonan Old Church

The Conbelin cross, Margam Stones Museum

On Bardsey

Romanesque tympanum, Llanbadarn Fawr (Powys)

Churchyard cross, Tremeirchion

On the way to Bwlch y Groes

Pilgrim cross, Bwlch y Groes

Shrine of St Winefride, Shrewsbury Abbey

St Winefride at Haughmond Abbey

View from the top of the rood loft stairs, Llandefalle

The running ornament, Llandefalle

The rood loft stairs, St Swithun's
Church, Brookthorpe

Memorial to Blessed William Davies,
Beaumaris

John Penry at the parish church of St Cadmarch, Llangammarch Wells

Cross fragment at Llangammarch Wells

At Tabernacle United Reformed Church, Llanfaches

On the Monmouthshire and Brecon Canal near Talybont-on-Usk

The Pales Meeting House

At the Putney Debates exhibition, St Mary's Church

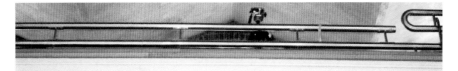

FOR REALLY I THINK THAT THE POOREST HE THAT IS IN ENGLAND HATH A LIFE TO LIVE AS THE GREATEST HE

COLONEL RAINSBOROUGH
1647

NEATH lie THE REMAIN
THOMAS CHARLES, B
ho died Oct.r 5, 1814, a
ble endeavours when in londo
y of the Holy Scriptures for
en he became the means
TISH and FOREIGN BIBL'S
r of the Welsh Circulating Cl
e Promoter of Sunday Schools
North Wales (the more immedi
urs for 30 years) will probably
trenuous exertions to promote
hrist till time shall be no m
elict of the above THOMAS
ed Oct.r 24, 1814, aged 61.
ssed of every natural endow

The grave of Thomas
Charles, Llanycil

At Llyn Tegid

Plaque commemorating
Thomas Jones, Berriew

ER GOGONIANT I DDUW
AC ER CÔF AM
Y PARCH THOMAS JONES O ABERRIW
1810 ~ 1849
Ef oedd y Cenhadwr cyntaf i'w anfon allan i Fryniau Khasi
yn India gan Gymdeithas Genhadol Eglwys Bresbyteraidd Cymru

TO THE GLORY OF GOD
AND IN MEMORY OF THE
REVEREND THOMAS JONES OF BERRIEW
1810 ~ 1849
He was the first missionary sent out to the Khasi Hills
in India by the Presbyterian Church of Wales

Hanover Chapel, Llanover

Towards Lancaut from Picturesque Piercefield

The ruins of St James' Church, Lancaut

The crossing, Ewenny Priory

At the site of St David's Church, Dylife

Stained-glass windows of slate quarrymen, Blaenau Ffestiniog

Inside the Gladstone Library

The Capel Celyn Memorial Chapel

On the Via Beata

St Tydfil in the Town Hall, Merthyr Tydfil

In the Taf Fechan
Nature Reserve

Ancient yew tree, St Tydecho's
Church, Llanymawddwy

St Samson on Caldey (left)
and St Mungo on High
Street, Glasgow

this distinction, at least as far as my own experience, is St Swithun's Church at Brookthorpe near Gloucester.[4] Here, too, I was free to climb the stairwell and look out over the body of the church from the empty doorway on the north side of the church, just to the west of the chancel arch.

I counted myself very fortunate that day at Llandefalle, and again at Brookthorpe, as although these internal staircases are often in evidence at medieval churches, often for reasons of safety they are not accessible to the visiting public. However, I was delighted to be able to carefully make my way to what would have been an additional storey to the building and see a view now lost to most of us as I looked across and down the church. At Llandefalle, this experience is heightened by the considerable size of this place of worship in a quiet hamlet about six miles to the north-east of Brecon.

However, if I had visited five hundred years ago, I would have found these stairs in regular use, as they led up to the rood loft and its large crucifix, this being flanked by statues of Our Lady and St John, with the whole ensemble being clearly visible from the lower level in the nave. At major church festivals, the faithful would mount the stairs, process past the rood to pray and kiss the feet of Christ and then descend back into the nave.[5]

In addition, the rood loft may also have been used as a place for proclaiming the Gospel, for musicians, and perhaps for rituals associated with the local saint's feast day.

Fortunately for us today and very much against the odds, a few rood lofts have survived in Welsh churches, with excellent examples at Llananno near Llandrindod Wells (*Llandrindod*), at Partrishow (*Merthyr Issui*) in the Black Mountains and, just a few miles from Llandefalle, at Llanfilo (although here the loft has undergone considerable restoration), but generally these three-dimensional structures have disappeared.

At St Matthew's[6] in Llandefalle, as at many churches, we don't know exactly when this happened but Theophilus Jones

(1758–1812), the notable historian of the former county of Brecknock, recorded in the early nineteenth century that some of the timber of the former rood loft had been used to create a gallery in the west end of the nave, so it had clearly gone by his time. (This has also long since been removed.) However, the lower part of the assemblage has at least in part survived. Here, on what is sometimes referred to as the 'running ornament', scaly-skinned dragons and lush foliage (apparently unrestored) continue to give us at least a two-dimensional hint of what must have been a glorious feature in this impressive church.

But even this is a rarity, and often the only evidence of the rood loft that survives in medieval churches in Wales and England is the doorway and stairs that would have led up to it, although these too were frequently lost during Victorian restorations to church buildings.[7] Even in these cases though, things may not be lost for ever. At the very picturesque St David's Old Church at Llanwrtyd, the staircase within the south wall was accidentally rediscovered by roofing contractors in 1968.[8]

Another feature relating to rood lofts that is worth looking out for in medieval churches in Wales and England is the small window that sometimes remains in the upper part of the south wall of the nave and which served to provide additional daylight for the crucifix. At Culmington in Shropshire this survives as it would have been when the loft was in place, whereas at Llangenny the same small window has long been blocked up, this being clearly visible from the outside of the church.

The memorial to Blessed William Davies, Church of Our Lady Queen of Martyrs, Beaumaris

OS: SH 606 762

The memorial to Blessed William Davies is a large bronze panel about one metre by two attached to the wall at the west end of the nave in this Roman Catholic church in a quiet street in Beaumaris on the island of Anglesey. In low relief, the dignified figure of Davies, a locally-born priest of the old faith, is shown flanked by various figures and awaiting his execution by the forces of the Tudor state in 1593; two of the men close to him, with their weapons and stern looks, are clearly part of the death squad. Meanwhile another holds his head in grief at the impending butchery, while a kneeling figure in front of the priest is shown accepting a Bible or prayer book from him. Two others look on, seemingly uncertain what to make of the momentous scene.

Above Davies' head is written *THY YOKE IS SWEET*, with *AND THY BURDEN IS LIGHT* following on at his feet, echoing the words of St Matthew's Gospel chapter 11, verse 30.[9] However, instead of a yoke around his neck, the prisoner has a hangman's noose for the first stage of his barbaric death by being hanged, drawn and quartered. The work of sculptor Ray Schofield (1948–2004), this remarkable piece was a very poignant thing to come across in this seaside town on the Menai Strait. Here the famous castle was the site of Davies' execution in 1593, following months of imprisonment in its dungeon.

Probably born in 1555 near what is now Colwyn Bay (*Bae Colwyn*), in his twenties he was ordained a priest, being one of several hundred young men from Wales and England who fled to the Continent in the reign of Elizabeth I to study at various colleges. These had been established to provide a seminary education and a route to ordination for those who remained faithful to the Roman Catholic Church.

Having returned to Wales, Davies engaged in the dangerous work of ministry among those who were prepared to risk the penalties for recusancy, that is, the fines imposed on lay people for failure to attend Anglican Holy Communion.

However, as a Catholic priest his activities were considered treasonous by the authorities in being counter to a statute of 1584. This required all such men to leave the country or to take the Oath of Supremacy by which they pledged their allegiance to the monarch as Supreme Governor of the Church of England.[10] This fundamental tenet of the new state church was, of course, quite unacceptable to those who considered the Pope to be the head of the church, hence Davies' execution on a charge of treason.

Beatified in 1987 by John Paul II, Davies was one of a wider group of Welsh Catholic opponents of the Church of England. Another close contemporary was Richard Gwyn (b. c.1537 in Llanidloes), schoolmaster and bard, who was executed in Wrexham in 1584.

Davies also involved himself in the writing of Catholic apologetics and is thought to have been the author of *Y Drych Cristianogawl*. This is believed to have been printed in secret in a cave near Llandudno in 1586 or 1587, making it the first book in the Welsh language to be printed in Wales.[11] In 2010, on a papal visit to the United Kingdom and on behalf of the people of Wales, Pope Benedict XVI was presented with a facsimile of the book produced by the conservator Julian Thomas at the National Library of Wales (*Llyfrgell Genedlaethol Cymru*) in Aberystwyth.

John Penry and Llangammarch Wells

OS: SN 935 473

The parish church of St Cadmarch at Llangammarch Wells is notable for its association with the Elizabethan puritan John Penry (1563–1593). A banner depicting Penry, made by the local Women's Institute, can be seen in the chancel. On the banner a young man in a Tudor doublet and hose stands in front of the house known as Cefn-brith, which is believed to have been Penry's birthplace and which still stands at about two miles to the south-west of the village. In his hands Penry clasps a Bible in Welsh.

However, the historic link between Penry and Llangammarch Wells cannot be definitively proved, but as a man of his father's name is known to have lived at Cefn-brith at the appropriate time, and suggestions in Penry's writings that he was familiar with the Brecon area, it is generally accepted that he was a son of this village situated just to the north-west of the steep escarpment of Mynydd Epynt.[12]

Thought to have been educated at the College of Christ of Brecknock,[13] Penry is known to have matriculated at Peterhouse, Cambridge, in 1580, taking his degree in 1584. By 1586 he was at St Alban's Hall, Oxford (this being later incorporated into Merton College), where he received his MA that year.

This choice of university would have been unusual for a young Welshman at the time, where studying as an undergraduate generally meant going up to Oxford[14] rather than the more distant seat of learning at Cambridge, but his decision is perhaps indicative of the considerable self-confidence that Penry would demonstrate in his short life. And although it is generally assumed that he and his family remained very traditional in their religious beliefs and practices before Penry went up to university, his studying in what was then a considerable centre for the new Protestant theology soon led to his adoption of what we would now call a puritan outlook on the Church of England, as established in the reign of Elizabeth I.

Penry's concerns, like others of a similar persuasion, included the opinion that the Sovereign should authorise the transition to a presbyterian model of government for the Church of which she was Supreme Governor, with bishops being replaced by a leadership shared between those in ministry and designated laymen. He also argued fiercely for better educated and resident clergy who would be competent to preach to their congregations. Above all, Penry wanted the laity to be instructed in the truths of the Bible which he believed people, and in particular his fellow countrymen, would welcome once they were taught effectively by godly ministers.

Writing several vociferous tracts, one of which, *The Aequity of an Humble Supplication*,[15] was presented to Parliament, Penry seems to have achieved a considerable notoriety before being executed for sedition under the Act of Uniformity of 1559 and the Act of 1580–1, 'preventing seditious words and rumours against the Queen'. However, he was largely forgotten after his death until his story was rediscovered in the nineteenth century by various historians of Welsh Nonconformity.[16]

History has also both corroborated and challenged Penry's views on the issues facing the Welsh Church of the late Elizabethan period. Contemporary documents reveal evidence which support his criticisms of clerical abuses and ignorance on the part of both clergy and laypeople. However, Penry has been shown to be unaware of (or perhaps choosing to disregard) the improvements which were being made in his own time, notably in the translation of the Bible into Welsh and its distribution to parish churches. This had been authorised by Act of Parliament in the early 1530s, with Welsh bishops and their counterpart in Hereford being commanded to ensure the law was implemented by St David's Day 1567. Moreover, although Penry made many protestations referring to Wales in his writings, it is likely that he never returned to his homeland after he had been awarded his MA at Oxford. Recent scholarship places him among the wide spectrum of puritanism in England but with little, if any, of his influence extending to Wales in his lifetime.[17]

In addition to the striking contemporary banner of Penry, St Cadmarch's Church also includes a feature which may well go back to the earliest years of worship on this site, with the remains of a wheel-headed cross being built into the exterior of the porch on the west side of the building. Thought to date from the ninth or tenth century, with its annulets, distinctive spiral and curious 'gingerbread man' appearing to run across the lower section, the cross incorporates designs that are found at only two other sites in Powys and nowhere else in Wales.[18]

CHAPTER 8

A life to live

THIS CHAPTER DEALS with four very different places that, each in their own way, can contribute to a fuller understanding of the complexities of the middle decades of the seventeenth century. This was a period of growing religious and political diversity – not only in Wales but also more widely in Britain – but was characterised, above all, by the Civil War which broke out in 1642 between King Charles and Parliament. This was then followed by the era of the Commonwealth, which was instituted after the execution of the king and the subsequent abolition of the monarchy and the House of Lords. A republican form of government which saw Oliver Cromwell rule as Lord Protector from 1653 to 1658, the Commonwealth remained in place until the restoration of the monarchy in 1660.

Firstly, the beginnings of Welsh Nonconformity[1] are discussed in relation to what is now Tabernacle United Reformed Church at Llanfaches, between Chepstow (*Casgwent*) and Newport. Here, the puritan impulse which had begun in the reign of Elizabeth I could no longer be contained, and the first congregation in Wales outside of the Church of England gathered, both in a practical and theological sense.

Then, as a reminder of the loyalty felt by many, certainly among the gentry, to the Established Anglican Church, the lives of twins Henry and Thomas Vaughan are considered using the Vaughan Walk in Talybont-on-Usk (*Tal-y-bont ar Wysg*) as a base. With their work ranging from poetry, for which they are most famous, to the practice of medicine, astronomy and early scientific experiments, both brothers took up arms in the Royalist forces. Well-connected by birth and in the social circles within which they moved, the Vaughans are a reminder that, however appealing the cause of political and religious change may seem to us who are used to a high degree of liberty and freedom of conscience, many people in Wales at that time remained conservative in their thinking.

Meanwhile, not far from the Vaughans beloved River Usk (*Afon Wysg*), by the 1650s early Quakers were beginning to meet in the hills of what was then the county of Radnorshire (*Sir Faesyfed*), and other areas along the border with England. Moving even further away from the Established Church than those who had gathered at Llanfaches, these Friends shunned the burying of their loved ones in the graveyards of parish churches and established their own simple burial grounds to which they would then add Meeting Houses, as at what became known as The Pales in the Llandrindod Wells area.

But Wales was not alone in these varying trends, whether leaning towards or away from the Established Church and the traditional social order. All had their counterparts in England, to say nothing of religious change and tensions within both Ireland and Scotland which were united, if only in name, under the Stuart crown. Hence, the final section is concerned with the Putney Debates held in 1647 in St Mary's Church in what was then a Thames-side village in Surrey. There, displayed on the south wall of the nave, are words spoken by Sir Thomas Rainsborough, one of the contributors to the proceedings: *FOR REALLY I THINK THAT THE POOREST HE THAT IS IN ENGLAND HATH A LIFE TO LIVE AS THE GREATEST HE.* This striking sentence certainly seems prophetic of later advances towards democracy, the equality of all before the law, and of belief in universal human rights.

In twenty-first-century Britain we take universal suffrage for granted and that the right to vote is not linked to wealth or property. We also have an expectation that we can choose and freely express our religious beliefs. However, these ideas were only beginning to be openly discussed in the seventeenth century, as demonstrated at Putney. Here, landed gentry such as Oliver Cromwell and his son-in-law Henry Ireton shared a platform with the more radical Levellers, resulting in debates and thinking that can seem strikingly modern.

Today, a permanent exhibition in the church serves as a reminder of the lasting impact of these tumultuous years and their legacy as regards the freedoms we enjoy in our own times, both in religion and political participation.

William Wroth and the Llanfaches Gathering

OS: ST 437 912

Llanfaches, in south-east Monmouthshire (*Sir Fynwy*), is situated in an area that has been very much shaped by its proximity to England. It surely isn't surprising that what has been described as 'the birthplace of Nonconformity in Wales'[2] had close connections with both London and Bristol when it came into being in the late 1630s.

With separatist congregations emerging in London by the 1590s and the considerable growth of puritanism in Bristol, both cities became sources of support for the extraordinary Gathering associated with the local parish church and its clergyman, William Wroth.

Born in the county and educated at Oxford, Wroth (1576–1641) appears to have experienced a profound religious conversion in about 1630, although it is unclear at just what time he came to Llanfaches where he was the rector. Clearly possessed of great gifts in preaching, he attracted growing numbers of people from a wide area to meetings held in the local churchyard. His activities also drew the attention of the Anglican authorities and Wroth was summoned to the Court of Convocation in 1638, where he appears to have submitted to ecclesiastical discipline and continued in his post. However, within a year Wroth seems to have relinquished his living, with the Llanfaches Gathering being formally instituted in 1639. At this event a contingent of supporters from Broadmead Baptist Church[3] in Bristol were present, and also Henry Jessey (1616–1663), the leader of a pioneering separatist group in London.

Dying in 1641 just before the outbreak of the Civil War, which he seems to have foreseen as both abhorrent but inevitable, Wroth was associated with younger puritan preachers whose work continued into the Commonwealth period. These included Walter Cradock (1610?–1659) who led the Llanfaches group after Wroth's death, and also Henry Walter (1611–1678), another Monmouthshire man. Walter would then go on to become an 'Approver' in south Wales in the enforcement of the Propagation Act of 1650,[4] this being legislation which aimed to root out clergymen who were unsympathetic to the Commonwealth cause. He also later became the puritan vicar of St Woolos' Church in Newport.[5]

Like me, you can sit on a bench outside Tabernacle United Reformed Church on the edge of the village of Llanfaches beside the A48 between Chepstow and Newport, and marvel at the momentous nature of what unfolded here. However, the chapel has only been at this point since 1802. In the earliest days, with the crowds presumably unable to gather in the churchyard half a mile away once Wroth was no longer the local clergyman, people would meet in homes until a place of worship was eventually built at Carrow Hill nearby. By the early eighteenth century, support for the chapel was in decline but a revival in interest and growing numbers led to the purchase, in 1798, of land for the current building, just a short distance from the site of Wroth's earliest Gathering in the 1630s.

Now a member of the Wales Synod of the United Reformed Church, Tabernacle celebrated its 325th anniversary in 2014.

The Vaughan Walk at Talybont-on-Usk

OS: SO 112 228

The Vaughan Walk at Talybont-on-Usk is a celebration of the lives of Henry and Thomas Vaughan, born at nearby Newton Farm (then *Trenewydd*) in 1621. It's a short waymarked trail around the village, taking in a section of an old tramroad,[6] then various paths across fields and eventually back to the Monmouthshire and Brecon Canal which is such a feature of the centre of Talybont. The walk also includes the Vaughan Garden, which highlights the interest of both brothers in traditional medicine and herbal remedies, and follows a series of wooden marker posts with short extracts of their poems on what are rather like old railway signals.[7]

Believed to have been identical twins, Thomas went on to become an Anglican priest, a notable alchemist, philosopher and early experimental scientist, whereas Henry, although practising as a doctor in the latter part of his life, is now famous internationally as one of the seventeenth-century school of metaphysical poets.[8]

However, the lives of both brothers were deeply affected by the events of the Civil War and the subsequent Commonwealth period. With both Henry and Thomas fighting for the royalist cause, and both of them deeply committed to the teachings and worship of the Church of England, they very much lamented the execution of the king in January 1649 and the zealously puritan nature of the government which followed.

Thomas, in particular, was affected by this in being one of many clergy in the Brecon area and beyond who were deprived of their livings as Anglican priests for continuing to use the liturgy and forms of worship as set out in the Book of Common Prayer. Living much of his life in London and Oxfordshire (contemporaries criticised him, probably rightly, for absenteeism), Thomas died in 1666. Meanwhile Henry continued to live in the Talybont area, finding himself surrounded by churches that had been closed, albeit temporarily, under the new regime.

But it is for their love of the natural world and their deeply spiritual religious faith that the Vaughan brothers are remembered and which is celebrated in the Vaughan Walk. At one of the marker posts, besides the little Caerfanell river,[9] are found Thomas' words:

> What a clear, running crystal here I find!
> Sure I will strive to gain so clear a mind![10]

Nearby, examples of Henry's work include gems such as:

> Follow the cry no more: there is
> An ancient way
> All strewed with flowers, and happiness
> And fresh as May.[11]

Henry Vaughan is buried about a mile from Talybont at the parish church of St Bridget at Llansantffraed where his twin was priest; his grave can be found at the top of the churchyard. When the church is open, a visitor area with information about the brothers is available inside. However, there is a book in the porch where all those who visit the grave are asked to leave their names, with previous visitors having included the war poet Siegfried Sassoon. Inspired by a visit in 1923, Sassoon went on to write 'At the grave of Henry Vaughan' a few weeks later.[12] Recitation of this poem now forms part of the commemoration of the older poet's life at Llansantffraed around the time of his birthday each year.

Thomas Vaughan is buried in the churchyard at Albury in Oxfordshire where he died, although the exact site of his grave is unknown.

The Pales Meeting House and Burial Ground

OS: SO 138 641

The Pales is tucked away on a very quiet lane on the western side of Radnor Forest (*Fforest Clud*), about a mile north of the village of Llandegley. Gifted to *Addoldai Cymru* (Welsh Religious Buildings Trust) after a period of uncertainty as to its future, this Quaker Meeting House is the oldest in Wales in continuous use, being built in about 1717. However, the land on which it stands was donated in 1673 for the purposes of establishing a burial ground in this area of Radnorshire for what was then a new religious group.[13] The pattern of providing a site for interments often preceded the building of a meeting house, as the early Quakers generally met outside or in homes.

With their strong belief in the equality of all before God, and their dislike of any ostentation or the costly monuments that were so often a feature of parish churches, the provision of burial grounds was a priority for Quakers from the mid-seventeenth century, although the very earliest interments are thought to have been in fields and orchards. In a similar vein, graves were often left unmarked, although when simple memorial stones did later come into use, these were generally uniform in size and shape. Interestingly, a purely numeric form of dating was generally used to give the date of birth and death of the deceased. The purpose of this was to avoid any reference to 'heathen' deities.

Quakers also considered a set funeral service as unnecessary and that all land belonged to God, hence their opposition to the notion of ground being specially consecrated which was clearly integral to interment in the existing cemeteries of parish churches. Ironically perhaps, the name The Pales is probably derived from the wooden fence, or palisade, which originally denoted the land set aside for burial when the cemetery here was first instituted.

The involvement of a parish priest in funerals also went

against the ideals of a movement which had no ordained clergy and in which any individual could respond to the divine inner light.

Perhaps surprisingly, the early Quakers do not seem to have faced any legal or ecclesiastical challenges to burying their dead in this manner. However, the new movement's burial practices did incur some opposition in the publications of the time: George Fox, born in Leicestershire and by tradition often seen as the founder of the group, is recorded as responding to his critics: 'How dare you say that we Bury our People like Dogs, because we cannot Bury them after the vain Pomps and Glory of the World?'[14]

Fox's three visits to Radnorshire must have had a formative influence on the emergence of the Society of Friends in the county and beyond, with the earliest Welsh Quaker usually considered to be John ap John (?1625–1697, also known as Siôn ap Siôn) of Wrexham, who converted to Quaker beliefs under the Englishman's influence, and subsequently often travelled with him in Wales.

However, the early years of the group are also now seen as more complex than having originated solely through Fox's leadership. Thus, the movement is increasingly thought of as developing from pre-existing radical religious groups, notably the Seekers, who can be dated back to the 1620s in the London area. In addition, individuals of varying puritan backgrounds became Friends.

Another Quaker burial ground (these were often originally known as 'gardens') which can be visited is one close to St Mary Redcliffe Church in central Bristol, where the former cemetery is now a community garden with the gravestones neatly placed together in a designated area under a rocky outcrop. With the land purchased in 1665, its original purpose continued until 1932. An information board at the site also gives details of the remains of a medieval hermitage close by. Certainly, an interesting spot in a busy modern city and an intriguing find for me as I made my way home from my pilgrimage to Brittany.[15]

In the 1870s, The Pales was the home of the American Yardley Warner and his English wife Anne Horne. With a school on the premises having been set up a few years earlier, Warner, who had been involved in educational work with freed American slaves, worked as the teacher. Returning to live in the USA in 1882, his model of The Pales Meeting House as Noah's Ark, made for the couple's young children, is now at the Museum of Old Domestic Life in Springfield, North Carolina.

The Putney Debates exhibition, St Mary's Church, Putney

OS: TQ 242 756

This unique exhibition has lots of information about the Putney Debates which took place here between 28 October and 9 November 1647. Although only the inaugural discussions were held at this riverside church (later sessions took place in the nearby lodgings of Thomas Grosvenor, the New Model Army's Quartermaster General of Foot), it now makes a fitting home to what is a very varied collection of material relevant to those extraordinary events. These include photos of the original transcripts of the debates, details about the wider context of contemporary Putney, and recordings of the views of historians and civil rights experts of our own times.

The Putney Debates belong to the particularly complex and troubled years of the later 1640s in which a vast array of opinions emerged as to how England and Wales should be governed, as well as what to do about the situation in largely Presbyterian Scotland and mainly Catholic Ireland. With King Charles having found himself unable to rule without Parliament, and his attempt at autocratic rule between 1629 and 1640 having failed, the Civil War broke out in 1642 hot on the heels of a major rebellion across the Irish Sea. Forever summed up and certainly greatly oversimplified as a dispute between Cavaliers and Roundheads, these islands were plunged into perhaps the most challenging period of early modern history.

The situation had been brewing for some time. Even in the reign of Elizabeth I, the queen had been irritated by the demands of a small but vocal puritan group in the House of Commons. However, with Parliament only sitting for quite short periods of time and then only for a matter of weeks at each session, this very resourceful monarch managed to keep the Commons in their place by careful management of her own and the nation's finances. However, the beginning of a new century and the arrival of a new king from Scotland led to rising tensions between the increasingly confident lower house and the crown. James VI / I was skilful enough to keep these at bay but his son, Charles, seen as dangerously close to Roman Catholicism and influenced by the absolutism of France and Spain, finally lost control of his kingdom.

Ultimately, all the very different opinions and views that were unleashed during the 1640s were irreconcilable, and the Putney Debates are a great illustration of that perhaps unfortunate fact.

Meanwhile, their location in Putney was because the New Model Army was based there. Formed to try to replace the traditional county and local militias that had been such a feature of the first round of the Civil War between 1642 and 1645, the New Model Army was intended to provide Parliament with a national force that was more consistently under its control. However, the men who made up the new regiments soon fell under the influence of political and religious ideas which were often much more radical than those of most of the parliamentary opposition to the king.

Such were the ideological differences that, against the backdrop of considerable arrears of pay for ordinary soldiers, a General Council of the Army was created with the debates taking place in this context. Perhaps surprisingly, not only were those involved not all members of the Army with two notable figures, John Wildman[16] and Maximilian Petty, being civilians, but even the lowest military ranks were represented by men known as Agitators. In a role rather similar to much later trade union shop stewards, the Agitators were often allied to the group known as the Levellers, with whom Wildman was very much associated.

With ideas as revolutionary as universal (male) suffrage being discussed, as well as freedom of speech and religious liberty, it was probably inevitable that the Putney Debates would not result in any clear way forward in the constitutional impasse in which all parties found themselves.

Eventually, the more conservative elements, led by Henry Ireton and Oliver Cromwell, ensured that the gathering was disbanded and the Agitators told to return to their regiments. Meanwhile, on 11 November, the king succeeded in escaping from Hampton Court Palace, where he was being held as a prisoner of the army, thus providing a fresh diversion in the ever-evolving story.

All the detail that we know of the proceedings at Putney is a result of transcripts made at the time by a team of stenographers under the leadership of twenty-four-year-old William Clarke. Clarke later wrote these up, but his work was forgotten until rediscovered in the library of Worcester College, Oxford, in 1890.[17]

Unfortunately, we don't know exactly who was present at the Debates in addition to the contributors named by Clarke (they included those denoted as 'Buff coat' and 'Bedfordshire Man') or whether key figures from Wales were among the gathering. However, Welsh radicals such as William Erbery (1604–1654), formerly the vicar of the parish of St Mary in Cardiff but, by 1638, obliged to resign following an appearance before the Court of High Commission,[18] were in the forefront of events. In Erbery's case this included becoming chaplain to a regiment in the New Model Army, a role which was seen as key in the dissemination of new political and religious ideas.

Taking part in earlier public debates in Oxford, as well as further discussions on the *Agreement of the People* that followed on from Putney in January 1648, Erbery is recorded as invoking the biblical John the Baptist, making interesting comments as to how Wales and the north would come to unsettle the relative conservatism of the south of England.[19]

In more recent years, the events of Occupy London in 2012 also led to discussions, known as the New Putney Debates, on the nature of democracy, social justice and civil rights in contemporary Britain. True to the freedom of discussion that characterised the New Model Army, this included a seminar on dissent and debate in the armed forces, organised by Veterans for Peace UK.[20]

CHAPTER 9

A double grandeur

IN HIS *OBSERVATIONS on the river Wye, and several parts of South Wales*,[1] William Gilpin (1724–1804) made some interesting comments about the lower Wye Valley. Although he was keen to publicise the picturesque beauty of the area, he also mentioned three scenes he had come across which were indicative of the early industrial revolution experienced in Britain in his lifetime.

Travelling in the summer of 1770 and going from Ross-on-Wye to Chepstow, he first noticed, at what is now Lower Lydbrook, the 'large wharf, where coals are shipped to Hereford', these being the product of the already centuries-old small-scale coal mines of the Forest of Dean. By Gilpin's time, the fuel they provided was heating homes in the growing urban centre that was the ancient cathedral city of Hereford.

Having continued on his trip and passing into Monmouthshire and so into Wales, Gilpin disembarked from his boat at Tintern (*Tyndryn*) and went on foot to the 'great iron-works; which introduce such noise and bustle into this region of tranquillity'. Here, too, he was observing a long-established enterprise that dated to the sixteenth century if not earlier, this being a centre for the forging of iron into wire.

But it's perhaps his comments part way along the journey, when he sees other ironworks at New Weir near Symonds Yat, that are most informative of Gilpin's outlook and probably that of other early tourists for whom he was writing. Of New Weir, Gilpin writes, the forge with its 'volume of thick smoke, thrown up at intervals as its fires receive fresh fuel' adds a 'double grandeur'[2] to the scene.

For in his quest for the picturesque Gilpin seems to have by no means objected to the presence of industry, albeit small-scale, in the wooded and still very rural landscape through which he passed. With his *Observations* becoming the first of many guidebooks that continue to be written about the lower Wye Valley and its attractions, Gilpin seems to have been content with the 'double grandeur' of scenic beauty alongside industrial processes, at least occasionally. However, Gilpin urged his readers, and potential future tourists to the area, to consider above all visiting the 'noble ruin of Tintern Abbey', which he described as 'the most beautiful and picturesque view on the river'.[3] Today's tourists and pilgrims may well agree with Gilpin on this point: the attractions of Tintern Abbey (*Abaty Tyndryn*), in spite of all the intrusions of modern life, remain great.

We also certainly have Gilpin to thank for drawing the attention of his readers to the wider landscape. For not only did he extol the value of leaving the river and walking the mile or so up to the ironworks on the little Angidy river (today, unlike in Gilpin's time, this is a very quiet place to visit), but also suggested forsaking one's tourist boat to walk to Chepstow along the scenic walkways created by the owners of the local Piercefield Estate.

But in encouraging people to explore the western, Welsh side of the River Wye (*Afon Gwy*), Gilpin seems to have been unaware of the interest of the eastern bank which is in Gloucestershire. Perhaps put off by the prospect of disembarking onto very deep and slippery mud, he makes no mention of St James' Church on the Lancaut peninsula.

We can perhaps forgive him this as St James' had only recently been abandoned as a parish church in Gilpin's time. However, today it a very scenic remnant of what was once a thriving medieval village. Hence, together with Tintern Abbey and the Piercefield walks, discussion of Lancaut forms the first section of this chapter.

But, whereas Gilpin and others sought to interpret what they saw of the Wye Valley in terms of its picturesque beauty, Wales was also being seen at this time as a destination not only for early tourists but also as a source of subjects for artists. Notable among these was J.M.W. Turner (1755–1851), who is considered to be Britain's finest painter of the Romantic school. Particularly fond of painting Welsh castles in the context of dramatic landscapes, and also occasionally including industrial scenes,[4] he also took some ruined ecclesiastical buildings as subjects, these including Tintern Abbey.

But Turner's only major study of a church interior that has remained in use as such (although this is only in part) is his painting of Ewenny Priory (*Priordy Ewenni*) near Bridgend (*Pen-y-bont*). This being the finest Romanesque church to survive in south Wales, it remains a fascinating place to visit for all sorts of reasons, not least its interpretation in art.

Of course, what the budding tourist industry on the lower Wye Valley and Turner's paintings have in common are the considerable changes that were occurring in Britain at the time. These included the expansion of industry, growing urbanisation and also the availability of leisure and travel to a wider section of society beyond the aristocracy whose preserve it had previously been. Now, not only could eighteenth-century visitors enjoy what has been described as the world's first package tours as they made their way from Ross-on-Wye to Chepstow, but a teenager of limited means could undertake several sketching tours in Wales, the fruit of which would propel him to the ranks of the world's most renowned artists.

The improvement of roads and communications more generally were certainly factors in both these cases, but another important issue was a greater appreciation of the beauty and historic sites that were available in Wales and, more widely, in Britain. This was, in part, a result of war and unrest on the continent of Europe, and especially the Napoleonic Wars that followed on from the French Revolution in 1789, events which hindered the undertaking of a 'grand tour' by wealthy young men.

But although Gilpin and Turner only witnessed what we would consider very small-scale industry, the second half of this chapter deals with churches situated where the considerable impact of industrial processes on the landscape is still very evident. These have, in my view, a special 'double grandeur' all of their own.

With both places having their origin possibly as far back as exploitation of resources by the Romans, the extraction of lead at Dylife in the Cambrian Mountains and the growth of slate mining at Blaenau Ffestiniog in north Wales make perhaps unusual places for a pilgrim to visit. However, with the former now having only the foundations of a church (together with its graveyard) in a largely abandoned village, whereas the latter is a thriving, contemporary parish church, both places merit exploration. In particular, they make interesting studies of how the Anglican church, in a Wales that was increasingly defined by its Nonconformity, adapted in the nineteenth century to the new centres of population that sprang up in response to large-scale industrialisation.

Picturesque Piercefield, Tintern and Lancaut

OS: SO 535 942 (for the car park in front of Chepstow Castle and the beginning of the Picturesque Piercefield walk)

The Piercefield Estate, situated just to the north of Chepstow and now in part occupied by Chepstow Racecourse, has a fascinating but problematic history. In the possession of the Walters, a local land-owning family, from the early fourteenth century until 1727, in 1740 it was bought by Valentine Morris, a sugar planter and slave owner from Antigua. On his death three years later it was inherited by his son, also Valentine Morris.

Morris then proceeded to create an ornamental walkway, leading from Piercefield[5] to Chepstow and also north towards Tintern. Designed to provide wide vistas of the lower reaches of the River Wye and the surrounding cliffs and woods, those visiting the estate were also able to view the medieval castle at Chepstow in its splendid position above the river, as well as the estuary of the Severn in the distance.

Probably originally created with the assistance of Richard Owen Cambridge, Piercefield and its walkway is now protected as a historic landscape; this is not only on account of its relatively recent history but also because of pre-historic earthworks at Piercefield Cliffs and Blackcliff Wood. These are believed to be the site of hillforts that indicate the importance of the area in the Iron Age. Meanwhile, the eighteenth-century walk, with its 'Grotto', 'Giants Cave' and 'Lover's Leap', has been re-invented as a contemporary attraction. And although the original would have been only for the enjoyment of Valentine Morris' guests and invited visitors, anyone is now welcome on the 'Walks through Piercefield Park'[6] as promoted by various local bodies involved in encouraging tourism.

However, the cost of developing and enhancing Piercefield eventually ruined Morris and he was forced to relinquish the estate and return to live on his plantation in the Caribbean. The land then passed through the hands of two different proprietors before being bought, in 1802, by Nathaniel Wells who was both a planter and slave owner and also the son of such a man and an enslaved woman, Juggy, who worked in his house. Wells went on to be a Justice of the Peace and Deputy Lieutenant (a ceremonial appointment made by the Crown) of Monmouthshire. A wealthy man, he continued to extend the Piercefield Estate and also to own slaves on the island of St Kitts. On the abolition of slavery within the British Empire in 1833, he was compensated under the terms of the

Act of Parliament of the time. Nevertheless, he remains a notable member of the early nineteenth-century Black British community in Georgian Wales.

Just to the north of the Piercefield Estate is the historic village of Tintern Parva, with the nearby Barbadoes Wood and Barbadoes Hill providing a reminder of the area's close association with the sugar plantations of the Caribbean. Generally known just as Tintern, it's full name (the small) reflects its amalgamation some time ago with the larger and now defunct parish of Chapel Hill in which the medieval abbey, for which the village is famous, was situated.

Founded in 1131, this was the first Cistercian religious house in Wales[7] and only the second in Britain as a whole. Its historic significance has been commemorated relatively recently in the site's inclusion in the eastern section of the Cistercian Way, a walking route which celebrates the importance of the order in the development of Wales in the later Middle Ages. Today, the ruined abbey, which is in the care of Cadw, is a notable visitor attraction and also the focus of a new local pilgrimage route known as the Marian Way.[8]

Yet contemporary tourists, whose cars and coaches fill Tintern's car parks, or who walk by on the Wye Valley Walk[9] are following in the great tradition of the Wye Tour. Originating in the eighteenth century, the travellers of the time would take a two-day boat excursion of about thirty-five miles from Ross-on-Wye in Herefordshire down to Chepstow. Along the way, as they admired the picturesque nature of the wooded hillsides, rocky outcrops and towering cliffs, they would stop and explore on foot, including here at Tintern Abbey.[10] Some would then leave their boats below the Lower Wyndcliff Wood and make their way up the steep path to 'Mr. Morris' improvements at Persfield',[11] following the walkway to Chepstow.

However, although the late eighteenth- and nineteenth-century visitors undoubtedly enjoyed seeing the Piercefield Estate, Tintern Abbey and the nearby ironworks, one thing the early tourists missed is the now ruined church of St James at Lancaut on the Gloucestershire side of the river. Finally abandoned in the mid-nineteenth century, the arches and empty window frames of the medieval building on its lonely peninsula created by a great loop in the river would surely have pleased those in search of the picturesque.[12]

Thought to be an early medieval Christian site dedicated to Cewydd and likely to be the 'lann ceuid' recorded in the *Book of Llandaff*,[13] it is one of just a handful of churches which may be associated with this sixth-century saint. These include the parish church at Cusop in Herefordshire and Kewstoke in Somerset[14] but whereas the original dedication, presuming such was the case, has been lost in both these places, it survives at the very fine parish church of St Cewydd at Disserth (*Diserth*)[15] and also at Aberedw, both in Powys.

The ruined church at Lancaut is also notable for its Romanesque lead font which is now in the Lady Chapel at Gloucester Cathedral. This artefact is one of six very similar surviving pieces – each cast from the same mould between about 1130 and 1140 – that can be found in Gloucestershire.[16]

A remnant of what was once a populous village, by the eighteenth century Lancaut had only two houses that were inhabited. Today, it makes a wonderfully atmospheric and secluded place to visit, being situated in a nature reserve of the same name. With its lovely ancient woodland, this is overseen by Gloucestershire Wildlife Trust.[17]

Sadly, there are no longer boat trips along this section of the Wye. Even Gilpin warned of the difficulties with the tide,[18] which only expert canoeists should attempt to deal with, and the treacherous mud of the river's banks below Tintern.[19] But it is possible to travel in the footsteps of the early tourists by taking the Picturesque Piercefield walk from Chepstow as far as the Eagle's Nest beyond Wyndcliff and then picking up the Wye Valley Walk as far as Tintern. There, the bridge which can be found a short distance upstream from the abbey can be used to cross the river and then climb up to the Offa's Dyke Path which goes through woodland before reaching Lancaut Lane in the village of Broadrock. From there, go along the lane and then take the clearly marked (although quite steep at times) footpath down to the ruined church. It's then possible to take the path just below the ruins that goes through the nature reserve, rejoining the Offa's Dyke Path just outside Woodcroft. However, this route takes you over a section where there has been a considerable landslide some years ago. This requires quite a bit of clambering over boulders, but is only about 30 metres in length. It is also quite stable and is clearly marked, but some walkers may prefer to return to Broadrock and on to Woodcroft and down to the old bridge over the Wye to Chepstow (the final section here is on the Gloucestershire Way) and then to the castle nearby.

Overall, this is quite an energetic day so some contemporary tourists and pilgrims seeking the Picturesque may prefer to use the local buses running between Chepstow and Tintern and divide the walk into two. Such a strategy may result in time to visit the former Benedictine priory which continues to serve as Chepstow's parish church. Dating to soon after the Norman Conquest, it retains many Romanesque features.

Ewenny Priory and J.M.W. Turner

OS: SS 912 778

Ewenny Priory was one of numerous places in Wales taken as a subject by Joseph Mallord William Turner, one of the leading painters of the Romantic tradition in British painting. Apparently undertaken without a commission, his watercolour *Transept of Ewenny Priory, Glamorganshire* was first exhibited in 1797 at the Royal Academy, the artist working from pencil sketches[20] made in 1795 and 1798 on two of the three sketching tours that he made in Wales when still a very young man. Compared at the time to the paintings of Rembrandt, it is considered to be one of his finest pieces and is now in the collection of the National Museum of Wales.[21]

As with others of his works, Turner's *Transept of Ewenny Priory* does not give the viewer a true picture of the proportions of his subject, with the painter having enhanced the size and impressiveness of the interior of the Norman church. He also depicts the building illuminated with what would be an unnatural degree of light, and has brought forward and shifted around an ancient tomb, thus giving it a prominence that it does not enjoy in reality.

Turner also added all sorts of details that presumably reflect how he found the building being used when he visited: a woman feeds chickens with grain held in her apron, another figure looking on. Meanwhile, a man ushers a pig through the wooden screen that divides the interior of the church.

In the foreground are more chickens and various agricultural implements, including an old henhouse and an upturned wheelbarrow, apparently discarded. It's all in marked contrast to the fine Romanesque features not only as shown in Turner's painting but to be seen in the building as it is today.

The contemporary visitor to Ewenny Priory can position themselves where the artist must have stood to make his initial sketches, at the north-west corner of the crossing where the main body of the church met the transept. Looking south-east, two round-headed arches that would originally have led to side chapels alongside the presbytery can be seen. Even by Turner's time these chapels appear to have been lost, with the arches also being considerably exaggerated in height in the painting. On the south wall of the transept, three windows (arranged one over two) continue to allow light to flood in, while a door on the west wall, shown as open in the painting, would have given access to the cloister.

Undoubtedly one of the finest examples of Romanesque ecclesiastical architecture that can still be seen in Wales, Ewenny Priory is thought to have been built in the early twelfth century by William de Londres, a Norman knight who had seized land in Glamorgan.

As in medieval times, the contemporary visitor to Ewenny Priory has to negotiate a quite complex building which serves three purposes. Before the Dissolution of the Monasteries (the Benedictine religious house here was suppressed in 1539), these were: parish worship by lay people in the nave, the main body of the church; the use of the transept, presbytery and side chapels in the offices said and sung by the monks; the domestic and administrative areas used by the religious order in the life of their community. However, the most important distinction, that of segregation between lay and monastic use, was made clear by a stone screen, known as the *pulpitum*, which stood at the east end of the nave.

These different uses are paralleled today; in place of the original *pulpitum* (only part of the lower section of this survives) a beautiful glass screen, designed by Swansea-based artist Alexander Beleschenko (1951–),[22] now divides the nave from the area beyond, which is in the care of Cadw.[23] These two sections house, respectively, the local parish church and a small museum area.

The third part of the site, consisting of the remains of the conventual buildings and some surviving fortifications, which are in part incorporated into a fine early nineteenth-century mansion, is privately owned. This house, possibly designed by the architect John Nash, is a successor to the one built by Sir Edward Carne, who acquired the site at the Dissolution.

St David's Church, Dylife

OS: SN 862 941

The site of the former St David's Church at Dylife in Powys is a rather bleak but somehow very poignant location.[24] Only the foundations of this parish church remain following its demolition in the 1960s, although the graveyard that surrounded it remains open to new burials. Together with the Star Inn[25] close by, the church is almost all that survives of a community that centred on the extraction and processing of the lead that was to be found in the surrounding hills.

St David's, opened in 1856, faced competition in the form of three pre-existing Nonconformist places of worship, these being a Methodist and also a Baptist chapel (opened in 1841 and 1852 respectively) as well as an Independent chapel established some time before.

Sited on land which, historically, was at the juncture of four ancient parishes, the development of the lead mines, and the boom in population which accompanied this, had unsettled a traditional sparsely-peopled upland economy. But it was probably the establishment of the Methodist and Baptist chapels which prompted a local campaign for the building of a new Anglican church to promote worship as according to the rites of the Established Church.

In addition to pubs, the church and the chapels, the village of Dylife also had several shops, a post office and a smithy, as well as housing for the workers and their families and a school for the children.[26] However, in a landscape deeply scarred by mining, and especially by the process of hushing, whereby vegetation was removed and the lead ore exposed by releasing torrents of water from temporary reservoirs, it is hard to imagine this place as home to several thousand people as well as the industrial and other buildings that have long-since disappeared.

St David's was built with funds provided through the Society for Promoting the Enlargement and Building of Churches and Chapels, which had been founded in 1818. Incorporated by an Act of Parliament of 1828, the Society received considerable sums of public money to promote the cause of building more Anglican churches in areas where the provision was inadequate, too distant, or where there were insufficient seats which could be occupied without charge. In some areas, such as at Dylife, the traditional structure of local parishes also failed to reflect settlements that had sprung up in the industrial era, and a new parish was created.

The designer of the church was the Scottish architect David Brandon (1813–1897) whose work led to the construction of a building of gothic design. His original plan, preserved in the library of Lambeth Palace in London, provided for a traditional pattern of nave, chancel, vestry and south porch on an east-west alignment just to the north of the road that went through the village. Referring to the pews, as indicated on his diagram, are the words 'ALL FREE'.

There is some evidence that the extraction of lead at Dylife may have been carried out by the Romans,[27] who were keen to exploit the natural resources of their province of Britannia. In addition, the outline of a small fort can be seen a few hundred metres south-west of the village at Pen-y-Crocbren.

However, although there seems to have been production on a small scale in the seventeenth and eighteenth centuries, it was only in the early nineteenth century that exploitation commenced on an industrial basis, reaching its height in the 1860s.

But unfortunately for the community at Dylife, this heyday of lead extraction was short-lived. Foreign competition, the high costs of processing and transport and the depletion of resources all contributed to a decline from the 1870s and the near-abandonment of the village by the early twentieth century. With little in the way of alternative employment, the workers and their families drifted away – the last marriage at St David's Church was in 1915 and the final christening in 1926. Meanwhile, the school was closed in 1925.

Although a few local private houses originated as workers' cottages, there is nothing left of the extensive buildings at the site. However, a few miles to the south-east and just below the dam that retains the waters of Llyn Clywedog can be found the Bryntail Lead Mine Buildings (*Adeiladau*

Mwynglawdd Plwm Bryntail), which are a Cadw property and can be visited.

Stained glass windows depicting slate quarrymen, St David's Church, Blaenau Ffestiniog

OS: SH 698 459

Until the mid-eighteenth century the area occupied by the town of Blaenau Ffestiniog, and its associated quarries and mines, were the *blaenau* (uplands) of the historic parish of Llan Ffestiniog. As such, it would have been a scene of rough and stony moorland pasture with *hafotai* [28]for summer grazing, together with a few isolated homesteads and some ancient paths and trackways. These would have connected it with the lowland farms around the main settlement and the local church about four miles to the south. To the north, a route over a mountain pass, which climbs to a height of 376 metres, led over the hills to Dolwyddelan and the valley of the River Lledr (*Afon Lledr*) and thence to the River Conwy.[29]

However, stained-glass windows depicting quarrymen in the Victorian church at Blaenau Ffestiniog provide a remarkable illustration of the natural resource which changed what had previously been a quiet place of marginal agriculture into a bustling town. Moreover, the surrounding landscape was transformed by the extraction, processing and transport of the slate which ran in rich veins underground. With both earlier open-cast mines and the vast underground caverns that were worked from the early nineteenth century producing huge quantities of waste, the town and its environs would surely have been almost unrecognisable to someone who had lived in the area in the pre-industrial period.

The slate deposits of north Wales were known to the Romans, who used it to roof their fort at Segontium near Caernarfon, and during the Middle Ages very small-scale production seems to have continued. But it was only in the eighteenth century that landowners began to appreciate the commercial benefits of allowing quarrying on their property in return for a share of the profits. This was encouraged by the growth of urban centres, with their demand for such a durable and waterproof building material, not only in Britain but in North America and around the world.

I first came across evidence for the trade in slate when I was several miles from the mines and quarries and down on the banks of the River Dwyryd (*Afon Dwyryd*) not far from where it joins the bigger River Glaslyn (*Afon Glaslyn*). There, close to Pont Tyddyn-Isaf, I saw the remains of the wharf that was constructed at the terminus of the tramroad that came down from Blaenau Ffestiniog. Here the slate was loaded on to barges for transport to Porthmadog 'and from there to the world', to quote a local man I met nearby that day.

But the use of the tramroad and wharf, built in the later eighteenth century, was superseded by the building of the Ffestiniog Railway in the 1830s, this allowing the slate to be moved directly and more easily to the bigger wharves at Porthmadog. The abolition, in the same decade, of the duty on slate carried by sea to other areas of Britain also benefited the industry in north Wales, leading to rising production and a growing workforce.

The three slate workers depicted in the very distinctive stained-glass windows at the parish church, representative of the many thousands earning their livelihood in the industry, would have been known as 'rockmen' and would have worked in small teams. Of the two in the left-hand window, one is using an air drill to make deep holes for the explosives that will help, once detonated, to release a large block of stone. Alongside him his co-worker gets ready to push the charge into the rock with a sturdy, wooden pole. Needless to say, this was very dangerous work, often on huge underground rock faces, and the man with the drill is depicted as steadied with a chain or rope.

Meanwhile, another of the team is shown splitting the rock into thin, usable slates of different sizes using a hammer and chisel in what is clearly an outdoor scene with the hills beyond. However, there would have been others in the group who would have cut the initial block, typically weighing two tons, into smaller pieces ready for splitting to a depth of about a sixth of an inch.

Apart from the highly-skilled 'rockmen' (who made up about half of the workforce), there were also many other very varied roles.[30] These included negotiating prices with the owners or managers of the mine, removing the unusable rock within which the slate was found and dealing with haulage, both inside the mine and in the transport of the finished product down to the coast.

St David's Church on Church Road in Blaenau Ffestiniog was built in 1842 at a cost of £2,000. This was given by Louisa Jane Oakely, who was the owner of the Oakely Quarries between 1835 and 1879. Living at nearby Plas Tan y Bwlch and tracing their descent from the Evans family who had been local landowners in the sixteenth century, the Oakelys had been able to consolidate their mining interests in the town in the early nineteenth century, enabling them to become the biggest slate producers in the area. With an annual income from the workings of between £8,000 to £10,000, combined with a philanthropic concern for the inhabitants of the growing town, Louisa was well-placed in every way to not only provide the church but also a vicarage and associated endowments worth £120 annually.

The church was also to be a parish church, with Blaenau Ffestiniog becoming a new church district in its own right, thus reducing the size of the historic parish centred at Llan Festiniog. In 1848, Mrs Oakely also provided a hospital for the workers and their families.

The stained-glass windows at the church date from the building's centenary in 1942 and are the work of Powell and

Sons. It's perhaps significant that the pneumatic drill depicted was a tool powered by compressed air, produced by this time by a diesel engine. Meanwhile, the worker shown splitting the slates is doing this in the traditional way, as this process was not mechanised until later in the twentieth century.

CHAPTER 10

Go ye into all the world

THE CHRISTIAN RELIGION has often been characterised as a missional faith. At the close of the Gospel of St Mark, the risen Christ appears to the disciples and commands them: 'Go ye into all the world, and preach the Gospel to every creature.'[1]

In the immediate post-biblical period, this was, indeed, the case with Christianity expanding rapidly, first around the eastern Mediterranean, and soon throughout all of the Roman Empire and beyond into much of the known world. Not only did this include a westward expansion, including the British Isles, but the new religion also spread eastwards to India and is also thought to have penetrated into what is now western China.

The early medieval period then saw the consolidation of the idea of Christendom in Europe, with secular rulers holding power in conjunction with the Church which was, at least in theory, still a unified whole. Within Christendom, all were considered to be within the fold of the faith, although the tiny numbers that made up the Jewish diaspora unsettled this stereotype.

Also, to the north the still pagan peoples of Scandinavia and the Baltic were gradually Christianised around the start of the second millennium, in some cases by what we would consider coercion. Meanwhile, to the south and east, the rise of Islam had checked the early prominence of the faith in north Africa and what we have come to call the Middle East.

However, the Reformation in the sixteenth century resulted in the situation whereby the Roman Catholic Church, and in particular the Society of Jesus, undertook what might be considered the first missionary movement of the modern age. For although Catholicism can be portrayed by some as an agent of conservatism in this period, in reality the challenge of such great religious change resulted not only in efforts to reconvert the Protestants of northern Europe but also in a renewal movement within the Catholic Church itself and a rediscovery of a biblical mandate to proclaim the gospel. This led to the remarkable work of Jesuit missions in the Far East, which also take a perhaps unexpected role in the background to the story of Robert Jermain Thomas (1839–1866), who went from the Monmouthshire village of Llanover (*Llanofer*) as a Christian missionary to China, and eventually to martyrdom in Korea.

Meanwhile, with improvements in navigation (Captain James Cook made his three voyages to the Pacific Ocean and Australasia between 1768 and 1779) and a need for new markets and sources of raw materials, the world was becoming a smaller place not only for those engaged in overseas mission but also those involved in commerce.

Moreover, as well as the considerable growth in international trade and the rise of a more industrialised economy, the Christian faith in Wales and England was also going through a time of considerable change. The Protestantism that had emerged at the time of the Reformation, and which had then progressed and diversified alongside the great political upheavals of the seventeenth century, had been re-energised in the second half of the eighteenth century by renewal both within the Church of England and beyond it. This led to an increased interest in the translation of the Bible and its accessibility to ordinary people, culminating in the founding of numerous Bible societies.

Alongside this was seen a great expansion in pioneering forms of mass education through the means of Sunday schools, which themselves were very much influenced by the

Circulating Schools as established by Griffith Jones (1684–1761) earlier in the eighteenth century.[2]

And so, this chapter begins with the story of Mary Jones, who has been described as perhaps the most well-known Welsh woman of all time. Her determined quest over the hills of north Wales for a Bible in her native language must be known to anyone who has ever attended Sunday school and to many others, too.

Our own quest then continues further afield. Prompted by a modest plaque on a chapel wall in mid Wales, our onward journey will take us, with local miller's son Thomas Jones (1819–1849), to the hills of north India. It's then back to south Wales for a short while, before leaving for China and Korea with Robert Jermain Thomas.

Mary Jones Pilgrim Centre, Llanycil, Bala

OS: SH 915 348

The Mary Jones Pilgrim Centre (*Canolfan Pererin Mary Jones*) is a visitor attraction and education centre housed in what was the parish church of St Beuno at Llanycil, about a mile from the town of Bala (*Y Bala*). Run by the Bible Society (and previously known as Mary Jones World), it celebrates the heart-warming determination of a young girl who, in 1800, walked 28 miles in order to purchase a Bible of her own.[3] With various displays and exhibits, children's activities and video material, the story of Mary Jones is used not only to illustrate the circumstances of Mary's own life and times, but also the ongoing work of the Bible Society in making the Christian scriptures more accessible and more widely available in our own day.

Mary Jones was a fifteen-year-old girl from a poor family (her parents worked as weavers, although her father died when she was very young) who lived in the village of Llanfihangel-y-Pennant. Having saved money over several years, she set out to buy a Bible (although she appears to have

been able to purchase three[4]) from the Reverend Thomas
Charles (1755–1814) who was then living and working in Bala
and involved in the Methodist movement in the area. Accounts
of just what happened vary, but it seems that when she arrived
at his home, Thomas Charles had no Bibles to sell but, within
a day or two, copies had been procured for Mary to take home.

The tale of Mary Jones is clearly a story with everything: an
enterprising young protagonist in challenging circumstances,
the scenery of north Wales, a kindly clergyman, and all in the
context of earnest religious faith and a walk that even today
is demanding.[5] Unsurprisingly, it was not long before the
story was popularised. One particularly enduring version, *The
Story of Mary Jones and her Bible* by Mary Emily Ropes, was
published in 1882 and remains in print.[6]

However, the story of Mary Jones also had a lasting impact
in that it seems to have been used by Thomas Charles to prevail
upon his contacts in London to make the Bible in Welsh more
readily available and at a reasonable price. In a letter of 1804
to Joseph Tarn, one of the founders of the British and Foreign
Bible Society that was established that year, he wrote 'how
young females in service have walked thirty miles to me with
only the bare hopes of obtaining a Bible each', a comment
which seems to refer to Mary Jones and perhaps others like
her.

Inaugurated with the particular aim of providing a more
plentiful supply of affordable Bibles for Wales and building
on the work of the existing Religious Tract Society, the British
and Foreign Bible Society soon became hugely influential
around the world in both the translation and distribution of
Bibles. Now known as the Bible Society and with the strap-line
'we offer the Bible to the world', it continues to promote a wide
range of materials to encourage engagement with the message
of the world's bestselling book, including operating the Mary
Jones Pilgrim Centre on the shores of Llyn Tegid.

But essential to an understanding of the significance of

Mary Jones is an appreciation that this young girl was literate and an avid reader of the Bible. Thought to already have been walking several miles on a regular basis in order to use a copy owned by a family with more means to buy one than did her own, Mary had learned to read as a younger child at a local Sunday school. This was one of several in the area run by teachers trained by Thomas Charles. Born into a family in very modest circumstances in Carmarthenshire, Charles had benefited from schooling at Llanddowror, the home of Griffith Jones, which had eventually led the younger man to Jesus College, Oxford.

Also influenced by the Sunday school movement founded by Robert Raikes (1736–1811) of Gloucester, Charles procured finance for his own schools from well-known philanthropists including William Wilberforce (1759–1833), and from 1798 was the agent in Wales for William Fox's (1736–1826) Sunday School Society.

St Beuno's Church at Llanycil makes a fitting home for the pilgrim centre. Historically the parish church of Bala, it was declared redundant in 2003, being then bought by the Bible Society in 2007. The scene of Thomas Charles' marriage, in 1783, to local woman and shopkeeper Sarah Jones, he is also buried in the churchyard. Although rebuilt in the nineteenth century, the church retains a few remnants of the earlier medieval building. This includes some reused Roman bricks and tiles which are thought to have come from the fort of Caer Gai,[7] the site of which is about four miles away near the south-west shore of Llyn Tegid and about a mile north of the village of Llanuwchllyn.

Commemorative plaque to Thomas Jones, Berriew

OS: SJ 193 002

Approaching the village of Berriew (*Aberriw*) in the old county of Montgomeryshire (*Sir Drefaldwyn*) and just three miles west of the border with England, it could be easy to miss the Jerusalem Calvinistic Methodist Chapel in the hamlet of Refail. However, the commemorative plaque in slate on the exterior wall of the chapel proclaims the extraordinary journey of Thomas Jones, 'the first missionary sent out to the Khasi Hills by the Presbyterian Church of Wales'.

The son of a miller at nearby Llifior Mill,[8] the chapel was yet to be built when Jones was a child, with the local Calvinistic Methodists then meeting at his parents' home. Undoubtedly his father's profession was a formative influence on the young man, who eventually also joined the family business. However, he would go on to be not only a pioneering missionary whose practical skills, ranging from carpentry to lime-mortar masonry and blacksmithing, endeared him to the local people, but also to distinguish himself in mastering their language. He would then proceed to commit this to a written form including translating several books and St Matthew's Gospel. And although there had been some earlier progress in putting the then largely pre-literate Khasi language into writing (the Baptist missionary William Carey had made use of the Bengali script of which the local people had no knowledge), it is as the father of the language, as written in the Western alphabet, that Jones' greatest achievement is seen.[9]

Perhaps receiving some early education at the village school, Thomas Jones later went to Bala to study at the theological college established there in 1837 by Lewis Edwards (1803–1887) and David Charles (1812–1878). Believing himself to have a vocation to the mission field, Jones was rejected by the London Missionary Society but then able to gain the support, in 1840, of the then recently-established Foreign Missionary Society which was based in Liverpool.

Arriving in what was then Calcutta (now Kolkata) in 1841, he and his wife Anne then made their way to Sohra, also known as Cherrapunji, in the East Khasi Hills (now in the Indian state of Meghalaya). In an area largely under the control of the

British East India Company, Jones' habit, very unusual at the time, of sharing his useful practical skills, combined with his linguistic talents, helped him to succeed in winning converts and establishing churches. This was in spite of the general opposition to Christian missionaries for which the Company (whose headquarters were in Calcutta) was renowned.[10]

However, first his child, and then, in 1846, his wife died. This tragic loss led to a situation where he took a second wife, a very young woman, without the approval of the Foreign Missionary Society, resulting in Jones losing their support. He continued to work independently but eventually died of malaria in 1849 at the age of 39. He is buried in the Scottish Cemetery in Kolkata.

Thomas and Anne Jones arrived in India at a time of great missionary activity in India. Much of this had originally been focused on providing churches and pastoral care for the employees and their families of the various West European trading companies that were operating in the region.

However, by the 1840s, concern about evangelising the native peoples of India was well-established, in what was predominantly a Hindu culture. But, by working with the Khasi people, Jones placed himself alongside a minority ethnic, aboriginal group who followed their own religious beliefs known as Niam Khasi.[11]

Living close to the border with what was then Burma (and with Sylhet, one of the centres of mission, within present-day Bangladesh) the culture, language and ethnicity of the Khasis was more akin to the people groups of south-east Asia than those of India. Interestingly, family life and inheritance among them were ordered on matrilineal lines, which is still the case today.

Other Welsh Calvinistic Methodist and Presbyterian missionaries followed in Thomas Jones' footsteps, with their work leading to the extraordinary situation whereby eighty per cent of the population of this area of India continue to identify as Christians and with the Presbyterian Church of India being predominant among them.[12]

This enduring legacy of the missionaries who came from distant Wales to the Khasi Hills has led to contemporary discussion and exploration of the cultural links between the two very different places. These have been celebrated in music by the Cardiff-based songwriter and multi-instrumentalist Gareth Bonello in his album *Sai-thaiň ki Sur* (the weaving of voices). In a similar vein, the Welsh and Khasi Cultural Dialogues project has used theatre and performance art to explore the relationship from Khasi, Indian and Welsh perspectives.[13]

In 2018 the Meghalaya state government instituted 22 June (this being the day that Thomas and Anne Jones arrived in Sohra) as Thomas Jones Day in recognition of the Welshman's very considerable achievements.[14]

Hanover Chapel and Robert Jermain Thomas

OS: SO 316 079

Hanover Chapel in Llanover was first established in 1744, with what is now a nearby private home being the congregation's first place of worship. Situated close to the historic Llanover estate, and now very much a place of pilgrimage for visiting Koreans,[15] the current chapel was built in 1839 although there was some refurbishment later in the nineteenth century. With galleries on three sides, still complete with the benches dating to when the building was originally constructed, the chapel is a Grade II listed building on account of the retention of a significant number of its early features.

However, the chapel is especially remarkable for its association with the missionary and martyr Robert Jermain Thomas, whose father was the minister there from 1848 to 1884. Born in Rhayader (*Rhaeadr Gwy*), where Robert Thomas senior served at the Tabernacle Congregational Chapel, the family moved to Monmouthshire when their son was nine years old. The younger Robert was then educated at the recently-established Llandovery College,[16] eventually completing his education by studying for the ministry at New College, London[17] where he excelled in Latin and Greek.

It was at New College that Thomas received what he believed was a missionary call to China. This led to him completing his ministerial studies, being ordained, and embarking for Shanghai, all within a few months in 1863, when he was only twenty-four years old. Perhaps even more significantly, Thomas also married at this time, his bride being twenty-six-year-old Caroline Godfrey, the daughter of a well-to-do Northamptonshire family who owned a country estate. Spending four months travelling together by sea to the Far East, his beloved Carrie was to die, following a miscarriage, in March 1865.

Perhaps burdened by both grief at his wife's death and frustration with his overall situation, Thomas then resigned from the London Missionary Society (under whose auspices he was working) and moved north, to the smaller city of Chefoo, which was one of the few ports open to European trade. Now usually known by its Chinese name of Yantai, he was able to gain employment there – it seems on account of his knowledge of local languages – in the offices of the Maritime Customs.

Not only did Thomas' move to Chefoo provide him with useful employment but he also came into contact with Alexander Williamson of the National Bible Society of Scotland[18] whom he was able to meet on a visit to Peking (now Beijing) and in whose company he made the acquaintance of two Korean traders. Noticing that these men wore crucifixes, Thomas learned something of the history of Catholicism in Korea and found himself increasingly drawn to the 'hermit kingdom'.

Koreans were forbidden any direct contact with Europeans. With the nation being a vassal state of China since the thirteenth century, they were allowed to trade only with the Chinese and then in just a few designated ports. However, once back Chefoo and, with Williamson's help, having acquired Bibles and other literature in Chinese, Thomas was able to distribute these on an illicit journey to the west coast of Korea in September 1865. Travelling across the Yellow Sea with two local men, this dangerous venture took place in the context of the extraordinary history of Catholicism in the region and, in particular, the Jesuit presence in the Far East.[19]

For although the Jesuits had engaged in missionary activity in China and Japan from the sixteenth century, they had never evangelised directly in Korea, which was often a pawn in relations between the two bigger and more powerful countries. But, when the Japanese invaded in 1592, their forces included soldiers who were part of the quite large Catholic community in Japan. This owed its origins to the ministry of the Jesuit, Francis Xavier (1506–1552), and may have numbered hundreds of thousands of people by the late sixteenth century. In particular, one of the generals of the Japanese forces, Augustine Konishi Yukinaga (1555–1600), who settled in Korea after the war ended in 1598, was even able to request that a priest be sent from Japan to minister among his countrymen in the occupied Korean peninsula. This led to the arrival of the Spanish Jesuit, Fr. Gregorio de Céspedes (1551–1611), who was permitted to stay in Korea for a year before both he and the general were summoned back to Japan by the Emperor. However, it remains unclear just how much contact de Céspedes had with the general population during his brief stay in the country.

Meanwhile, some Korean prisoners seized in the war had been enslaved and taken to Japan, where some of them came into contact with the Jesuits and were converted to Roman Catholicism. These included Vincent Kwŏn, who trained as a Jesuit and was martyred in Japan in 1626.

For the following century or so, the extent of the Christian presence in Korea remains uncertain, although some Jesuit writings in Chinese were available among Confucian scholars who were able to read them.[20] This led to the extraordinary story of the well-connected Yi Sŭng-hun (1756–1801) and his cousin, Yi Pyŏk (1754–85), who came across and studied the text, *The True Meaning of the Lord of Heaven*, written about two hundred years earlier by the Jesuit missionary to China, Matteo Ricci (1552–1610). Written in classical Chinese and putting the case for the Christian faith in the context of Confucianism and in the form of a dialogue, the two young men were so greatly challenged by what they read that Yi Sŭng-hun sought permission to travel to Beijing to receive baptism. When he later returned to Korea, a group of converts began to gather around the two cousins, leading to the number of Catholics there growing to perhaps four thousand by the 1790s.

Although, at first, they remained an autonomous lay-led church beyond any episcopal oversight, in 1794 the Chinese priest James Ti-Yu was sent to minister among them. Unfortunately, though, the group began to attract the attention of the Korean authorities, who opposed any contact with what was seen as alien Western thought. Fierce persecution then broke out, resulting in the martyrdom of James Ti-Yu and of Yi Sŭng-hun and others by beheading in 1801.

Hostility to the Christian faith continued until the 1860s, but it was at this point that the story of Robert Jermain Thomas overlapped with that of the persecuted Korean Catholics. Keen to make a second missionary journey from Chefoo to the west coast of Korea, Thomas was offered the opportunity to travel as interpreter on a French vessel which was to be sent to protest against the then recent execution of nine French missionary priests. But the delay in sending this ship and uncertainty over whether Thomas was authorised by the London Missionary Society (with whom he had re-established relations) led to him accepting a passage on an armed merchant vessel, the *General Sherman*. Keen to make trading links with Korea, the American owner and captain of the *General Sherman* approached the coast without permission and then made his way up the River

Taedong towards Pyongyang. Receiving numerous warnings from officials, the schooner eventually ran aground, leading to a violent incident in which local people were fired on and all those on the *General Sherman* were killed. This included Thomas, who appears to have been cut down as he tried to make his way ashore, but not before he had placed a Bible in the hands of a local Korean.[21]

Although he died when still such a young man, and with having made only two brief journeys to Korea with very little in the way of success, Thomas is seen as the founding martyr of Protestant Christianity in the country. Divided since the end of the Second World War into North and South Korea, the latter is considered by some to be the most Christianised nation in the world, whereas in North Korea religious faith is harshly persecuted.[22]

Another twist, though, to this story is that Thomas was not the first Protestant missionary to visit Korea. In the 1830s, the German Karl Gützlaff (1803–1851), who had worked for the Netherlands Missionary Society and then independently, was able to travel along the coast of Korea and distribute Bibles and other literature in Chinese.[23]

CHAPTER 11

The twentieth century and the new millennium

THE ISSUE OF slavery and the slave trade within the British Empire has already been touched upon in relation to the Piercefield Estate near Chepstow but, in selecting Gladstone's Library in Flintshire as one of the places to be discussed in this chapter, it is apt to return to what has become an ongoing debate in the contemporary campaign for greater racial justice and the Black Lives Matter movement. For W.E. Gladstone (1809–1898), perhaps the most distinguished and best-known figure in nineteenth-century British politics, at first took an ambivalent view of the abolition of slavery. As a young man he supported only a gradual emancipation and was instrumental in securing the greatest sum of compensation paid to any British slave owner under the terms of the Slavery Abolition Act of 1833, this being to his father, John Gladstone (1764–1851), who had extensive interests in Jamaica and Guyana.

However, in the course of his long life, Gladstone seems to have undergone a considerable change of heart, later acknowledging that he had been on the wrong side of the argument and that those who supported immediate abolition had been in the right.

But, above all, Gladstone was a devout Christian who, in founding St Deiniol's Residential Library (as it was originally named), created a legacy which endures to this day as testimony to the value of an informed religious faith, able to engage with the society which surrounds it and of which it is a part.

Another very complex nineteenth-century debate was what to do about British rule in Ireland. This, too, has evolved into discussions in our own times around the future of the island of Ireland, which in Gladstone's day formed part of Great Britain and was ruled from Westminster. However, from the late 1860s and to the end of his political career, Gladstone pursued the often unpopular cause of Home Rule, something that he failed to achieve in his lifetime.

Moreover, the very entrenched and ultimately irreconcilable views on the Irish question continued unresolved at the outbreak of the Great War and were to form the backdrop to the nationalist Easter Rising of 1916, which had as its aim the establishment of an independent republic. The imposition of martial law and the suppression of the rebellion by the British army resulted in the taking of numerous prisoners, many of whom were taken to camps in Wales and England. One of these was sited at Frongoch which today is about two miles below the dam which holds back the waters of the Llyn Celyn reservoir. The controversy surrounding the construction of the dam in the late 1950s, the ensuant loss of the Welsh-speaking village of Capel Celyn and the building of a Memorial Chapel form the subject of the second section of this chapter.

Meanwhile, alongside the A4212, an information board gives details of how 1,800 Irishmen were confined here for six months in wooden huts and a former distillery that made up the Frongoch Prison Camp (*Gwersyll Carchar Frongoch, Campa Géibhinn Frongoch*). In 2016, a memorial to the camp, and in particular the men of Galway who were imprisoned there, was added alongside the information board. (Nothing is now visible of the original buildings.)

As very much suggested at Frongoch, there are certainly comparisons that can be drawn between Irish and Welsh nationalism – the former becoming an increasingly strident cause in the nineteenth century, eventually leading to the founding of an independent state in the south of Ireland in 1922. Meanwhile, later in the twentieth century, and perhaps partly in response to the imposition of the dam at Llyn Celyn following an Act of Parliament, calls for some measure of devolved rule in Wales, and even for independence, also became an essential part of the landscape of Welsh political life.

However, to return to Gladstone, one of his successes was to secure the Disestablishment of the Anglican Church of Ireland by an Act of Parliament of 1869. Although this clearly provided a precedent for the same to be accomplished in Wales in 1920,[1] the pre-dominance of Catholicism in much of Ireland provided a very different setting to that of Wales.

Meanwhile, continuing poverty in Ireland, as exemplified by the Great Famine of 1845–52, led to considerable levels of emigration to Wales and England. This resulted in a changing religious complexion in many towns and cities and contributed to an increasingly confident Roman Catholic community in both countries in the twentieth century. The foundation of Our Lady of Fátima Catholic Church at Bala after the Second World War, discussed in the third section of this chapter, is in this context.

A glimpse into some very serious politics has formed this introduction, perhaps as Gladstone himself would have appreciated. But this chapter also touches upon hopes and, indeed, prayers at the beginning of a new millennium as demonstrated in the setting up of the Via Beata pilgrim route across Wales and England. This project is outlined in the final section.

Gladstone's Library, Hawarden

OS: SJ 315 659

Gladstone's Library in the Flintshire village of Hawarden (*Penarlâg*) was originally known by the name St Deiniol's

Residential Library, this being the choice of its founder and benefactor W.E. Gladstone. Eventually becoming known as St Deiniol's Library, the current name, perhaps chosen to appeal to a wider public, has been in use since 2010.

Gladstone, who was prime minister for a total of twelve years over a still unique four terms, had married into the Glynne family of nearby Hawarden Castle, an eighteenth-century mansion which took its name from the earlier ruined Norman castle which is still to be found on the Hawarden Estate. With the male line of his wife's family having died out, he and Catherine Glynne went on to have eight children. Today the estate still belongs to the Gladstone family.

At the family home at *new* Hawarden Castle, and with what must have been a very busy public and private life, Gladstone had a new wing constructed, which he called the Temple of Peace. This was built to house his vast collection of books and provide a haven for reading and study. But aware that most people did not have access to such a resource, Gladstone permitted local scholars and students to use his extensive personal library.

Then, in 1889 and towards the end of his long life, he set about creating a more lasting home for his collection which would make it as accessible as possible to anyone who wanted to use his books for study. It is said that he transported twenty-five thousand of these books himself – in a wheelbarrow and with the help of a valet and one of his daughters – from Hawarden Castle to the simple buildings within which the new library was first housed. Moreover, those students and readers who needed accomodation were able to lodge in an inexpensive hostel nearby, these arrangements then being formalised in a trust which Gladstone endowed with £40,000.

With Gladstone dying in 1898, public funds were raised to augment his endowment and provide a lasting and purpose-built home for what would be a National Gladstone Memorial. This resulted in the opening of the current Jacobethan-style building with its library range and offices and also a residential wing, which was financed by the Gladstone family.

Officially opened in 1902 at the very beginning of the twentieth century, the library has continued to reflect Gladstone's interest in religion, philosophy, history and literature and, perhaps above all, his deep religious faith. With a small chapel at the heart of the building, a 'brief gathering' is held early each day 'with a simple sharing of bread and wine according to an open and inclusive Christian tradition'. True to its founder's original intentions, the library also continues to offer reasonably-priced accomodation and also allows readers, whether resident or not, to register to use the facilities and study without charge and without having to meet a required academic level. It is also possible for tourists, and pilgrims, to make a brief visit to the splendid main reading room at set times most days, which I was able to do as I made my way north to the Isle of Man.

Gladstone's Library is also close to the local parish church of St Deiniol, where Gladstone and his wife Catherine are buried and from which its original name was derived.

In about 525 Deiniol is believed to have established a simple cell close to the Menai Strait at its narrowest point, this then evolving into St Deiniol's Cathedral (*Cadeirlan Deiniol Sant*) at Bangor, which was consecrated in about 546 with him as the first bishop.

However, Deiniol seems to have also been active across north-east Wales with several churches in this area, as well as to the south and along the border with England, being dedicated to him.

At Hawarden, a sixteenth-century house known as St Deiniol's Ash, situated a short distance from the church, is by tradition seen as being at the location where the saint first placed his episcopal staff, after coming ashore from the River Dee (*Afon Dyfrdwy*).

Capel Celyn Memorial Chapel

OS: SH 848 413

The Capel Celyn Memorial Chapel (*Cofeb Capel Celyn*) is on the north-east shore of the Llyn Celyn reservoir and is accessed by a short, grassy lane that leads from the A4212 as it makes its way from Bala to Trawsfynydd. Completed in 1967, the chapel commemorates the loss of the village of Capel Celyn when the reservoir was created in the late 1950s and early 1960s in order to increase the water supply to the city of Liverpool.

The area on which the chapel stands was originally designated as a place for the re-interment of the village's deceased who had been buried in the graveyard of the Calvinistic Methodist place of worship which had been constructed in 1820 and rebuilt in 1892. Along with other buildings in Capel Celyn, including a school and a post office, the chapel was demolished in 1964 as the dam that held back the water of the Afon Tryweryn took shape and the valley through which the river flowed was slowly flooded.

With local people being given the choice of having their dead re-interred at other local cemeteries (this only occurred in two cases) or at the site of the Memorial Chapel, or having relatives' graves left *in situ* and sealed with concrete,[2] this place is a poignant reminder not only of a lost landscape but of the lives that were lived there and had been lived there for centuries.[3]

Primarily a farming community, about a dozen farmhouses were lost as well as the agricultural land that surrounded them. The Memorial Chapel itself was built on the site of the former farm of Gwern Delwau whose stones, as well as those from other buildings including the original chapel, were used to construct the new memorial.

Today, gravestones removed from the former cemetery are placed along the boundary walls of several small enclosures that have been made between the Memorial Chapel and the road. Like tiny fields, but with walls made of quite large boulders, they are a reminder of what has been lost for ever. Among them can be found the original dedication stone of the Calvinistic Methodist chapel.

However, as well as the very human story of the end of a close-knit community and the land on which it depended, Capel Celyn has acquired a far greater significance, not only as regards the struggle of local people to prevent the creation of the reservoir but also in the loss of a village whose residents were entirely Welsh speaking.

Shocking though this may seem now, the Corporation of Liverpool was able to push a private member's bill, the Treweryn Reservoir Bill, through Parliament at Westminster.

Although thirty-five out of thirty-six Welsh MPs opposed the bill (David Llywelyn MP, represnting Cardiff North abstained), it was passed by Harold Macmillan's Conservative government in 1957. Proceeding without any consultation with the people of Capel Celyn or any requirement to meet planning regulations within Wales, Liverpool Corporation was then able to compulsorily purchase the land in the Treweryn valley and build the dam.

Needless to say, the people of Capel Celyn mounted a strong campaign to save their village with the Capel Celyn Defence Committee being set up, with a branch in Liverpool, to oppose the drowning of their homes.[4] With numerous protests against the scheme, including a demonstation in the northern city by the entire population of the village apart from a tiny baby, the huge efforts made to oppose the creation of the reservoir received considerable support in Wales and are now seen by many as a turning point in the cause of Welsh nationalism. With the then leader of Plaid Cymru, Gwynfor Evans (1912– 2005),[5] being closely involved in the campaign against Liverpool Corporation, the ease with which this English local authority was able to implement its plans led to a greater realisation that Wales needed not only stronger representation at Westminster but also contributed to growing support for Welsh independence.

Designed by the sculptor Robert Lambert Gapper (1897–1984) of Aberystwyth, the Capel Celyn Memorial Chapel, which is owned by Welsh Water (*Dŵr Cymru*), was closed for several years due to structural problems but was then re-opened following a programme of refurbishment. However, the very poignant memorial garden has always been accessible.

In 2005 Liverpool City Council issued an apology, stating: 'We realise the hurt of forty years ago when the Tryweryn Valley was transformed into a reservoir to help meet the water needs of Liverpool.' However, the story of Capel Celyn remains an emotive issue.[6]

There is also another memorial associated with the creation of the reservoir, not far from the dam and about two miles back down the A4212 towards Bala. Here, a commemorative plaque records an earlier period in Capel Celyn's history, that of the farmstead Hafod Fadog which was used as a meeting house by Quakers in the seventeenth and eighteenth centuries. This building was among those that were lost when the valley was drowned, as was a cemetery associated with it. The plaque explains how early Quakers from this area were among those who emigrated to Pennsylvania 'to seek freedom of worship in the new world'.

Our Lady of Fátima Catholic Church, Bala

OS: SH 925 359

'Many Catholics are unable to go on a pilgrimage to Fátima in Portugal, so every year pilgrims visit Fátima here in Bala.'[7]

In a place which has been so significant in the history of Welsh Nonconformity, it may seem surprising to find not only a thriving Catholic parish but also the first church in the world, outside of Portugal, to be dedicated to Our Lady of Fátima, but such is the case at Bala. With the entrance tucked away in a small courtyard off the A494 as it goes through the centre of the town, this small place of worship in southern Snowdonia is a remarkable testimony to the resilience of the Catholic faith in Wales.

As the church's website states, it is a considerable journey, and in more ways than one, from Bala to Fátima, a town in central Portugal to which pilgrims come from all over the world.[8]

However, the small number of Catholic parishioners living in Bala after the Second World War were encouraged to pray for the provision of a church building through the ministry of the Dominican priest, Father James Koenen. Arriving in the town in 1946, the Dutchman had a particular devotion to the cult of Mary at Fátima and urged the faithful to pray to her for money to buy a suitable site.

At that time needing to walk several miles to a nearby convent in order to attend Mass, local Catholics took the cause to their hearts and were soon able to buy a former business premises (part of the building had previously been used as a fish and chip shop) to convert into a church and presbytery. This was opened as a place of worship in 1948, with Father James and his congregation having carried out much of the building work themselves.

Although the then bishop of the Diocese of Menevia, John Petit (1895–1973), had originally intended that the new place of worship be consecrated to a Welsh saint, the view of Father James that the dedication should be to Our Lady of Fátima eventually prevailed, and so Portugal came to Wales!

The story of the three illiterate peasant children who, beginning in 1916, saw repeated visions of an angel and of Mary, the mother of Jesus, as they watched over the family's sheep on a quiet hillside remains a powerful one. The two younger children, siblings Francisco and Jacinta Marto, then aged nine and seven, sadly died young in the Spanish Flu pandemic which followed the Great War. However, as growing numbers of pilgrims were increasingly drawn to Fátima, their cousin, Lucia dos Santos (1907–2005), was taken from the village in 1921 in order to attend a school run by the Sisters of St Dorothy, eventually becoming a Carmelite nun.

The visions experienced by the children were very much against the backdrop of the war in Europe and the desire for an end to hostilities. They were repeatedly told by Mary to pray the rosary so as to bring about peace, to do penance for the sins of others, and even given a glimpse of the torment of sinners in hell. The fall of Russia to an atheistic power, a later war and an attempt on the life of the Pope, were also included in the words that were entrusted to them.

Perhaps remarkably to us in our very different world, the children seem to have taken what they saw and heard very seriously, and also attempted at first to keep what they had experienced to themselves. Inevitably, though, stories soon began to circulate and questions were asked about whether the visions could be considered to be genuine.

However, after decades of discussion and debate, the process by which the children would be officially recognised as saints was begun by Pope Francis on the centenary of the visions. This was seen as an acknowledgement that Pope John Paul ll's survival following an assassination attempt in 1981 was due to the intercession of Francisco, Jacinta and Lucia, and so provided grounds for their canonisation.

Meanwhile, back in Bala, the new millennium was marked by the building of a beautiful new shrine to Our Lady of Fátima situated in a small extension at the back of the church. With the design, materials and workmanship all coming from within Wales, the stained-glass window incorporated within it was designed by Swansea-based Loreto Sister, Jen Bromham.[9] Entitled *The Miracle of the Spinning Sun*, it is a representation of one of the visions seen by the three children and other witnesses, whereby the sun appeared to dance in the sky.[10]

The Cross at Ffald-y-Brenin and the Via Beata

OS: SN 047 352

The Via Beata, or Way of Blessing, is a new pilgrimage route which crosses Wales and England at the widest point, from Lowestoft in Suffolk to St Davids in Pembrokeshire.[11]

Devised as a celebration of the beginning of the third millenium since the birth of Christ, it is an ongoing project which includes works of art, called 'way-stations', which are inspired by the Christian faith. At the time of writing, the hope is that the number of these within Wales will increase, including the provision of one at St Davids Cathedral (*Eglwys Gadeiriol Tyddewi*).

Meanwhile, with the trail having been built up over several years from its eastern extremity on the North Sea, the Cross at Ffald-y-Brenin in the Gwaun valley (*Cwm Gwaun*) is currently the most westerly of the way-stations. Situated on a small outcrop on a steep hillside, it is not only a focal point within Ffald-y-Brenin, but also has magnificent views over a lovely wooded landscape and beyond to the Irish Sea. From the Cross, it's a good day's walk across the Preseli Hills (*Mynyddoedd y Preseli*) to St Davids and the end of the Via Beata.

Founded in the 1980s on the site of pre-existing farm buildings, Ffald-y-Brenin is a Christian retreat centre which is known around the world. With a spirituality that draws on factors as varied as the Welsh chapel tradition, monastic routines of prayer, twentieth-century renewal movements and the lives of the early saints (Brynach is thought to have prayed with his arms outstretched on the summit of a nearby hill), it is unique within Wales.

Another very different way-station on the Via Beata is in the town of Hay-on-Wye (*Y Gelli Gandryll),* on the border with England and the county of Herefordshire. Known as 'the town of books' because of the range and number of second-hand book shops within one quite small place, here the Way of Blessing leads the pilgrim to the words of Simon Peter to Jesus in St John's Gospel: 'Lord, to whom shall we go? You have the words of eternal life' / '*Arglwydd, at bwy yr awn ni? Y mae geiriau bywyd tragwyddol gennyt ti.*'[12] Found in a small public space alongside the Wye and close to the road bridge over the river, it takes the form of a bench with incised lettering designed by Will Spankie, a stone carver and letter cutter.

Meanwhile, if you are vigilant in the very quiet places that the Via Beata passes through in mid Wales, you might see one of the discs that denotes this Way of Blessing, as I did on a lonely forest track in the Llandovery area.

CHAPTER 12

The early saints revisited

THIS FINAL CHAPTER takes as its inspiration various contemporary interpretations of early saints and their lives. These include not only examples of art and literature but also current academic research, and was prompted by walking on pilgrimage through the south Wales town of Merthyr Tydfil (*Merthyr Tudful*). There, where the town's name commemorates St Tydfil's death,[1] one might reasonably expect her to be long gone. However, Tydfil is very much with us and is not only depicted on all the local street signs but also features in a book of short stories by the German-born author and historian, Imogen Ria Herrad.

Another saint born in Wales who is doing very well is St Samson of Dol, whose statue can be found on Caldey Island (*Ynys Bŷr*) near Tenby (*Dinbych-y-Pysgod*). There, the religious community who call the island home continue the tradition of monastic life in which the saint himself played a part around fifteen hundred years ago.

But, in addition to being portrayed in visual art, Samson is very much under scrutiny in academic discussion and research as far away as Australia, as he has the great advantage in being one of the very few early saints whose story, written reasonably soon after he died, has survived into our own times.

Although in no way comparable to a modern autobiography, the anonymous *Life of St Samson of Dol*[2] is a close to unique glimpse into the sixth-century Church in south Wales and the south-west of England, with the Latin text continuing to stimulate debate and add to our knowledge of the early medieval period in north-western Europe. Here, I have taken short extracts (in translation) from this extraordinary document to tell a little of what we know of this son of west Wales.

In Scotland too, St Mungo can be found in very striking street art where he lives on in central Glasgow (*Glaschú*), the city of which he is patron saint. But, perhaps confusingly, he is a man who goes by two names. Called *Kentigern* by his parents, the saint later acquired the ecclesiastical nickname *Mungo*, by which he is often still referred. However, he is also the putative founder of St Asaph's Cathedral (*Cadeirlan Llanelwy*) and his life, including his connections with north Wales, has been the subject of study in recent years in the USA.

But not everyone wants or enjoys the limelight, and so the chapter concludes with how traditions surrounding St Tydecho, who is barely known outside his home territory in southern Snowdonia, are being preserved in the landscape around the village of Llanymawddwy, in the upper reaches of the Dyfi Valley.

St Tydfil in Merthyr Tydfil

OS: SO 050 063

It is quite easy to find Tydfil in the town which not only has taken her name but also venerates her memory. Her image seems to be everywhere, including on a roundel inside the imposing town hall. There, she takes her place alongside other notable figures in the area's history including Richard Trevithick (1771–1833), whose locomotive made the first steam-powered journey in the world on a local tramroad, and Keir Hardie (1856–1915), the founder of the Labour Party and also MP for Merthyr Tydfil in the early twentieth century.

But it's in literature that a particularly interesting interpretation of this south Wales saint can be discovered in *The Woman who Loved an Octopus and other Saints' Tales* by

Imogen Ria Herrad, with 'Tydfil' being the final piece in a highly imaginative and very entertaining book. Taking what are often little more than legends surrounding the names of thirteen early female saints,[3] the author uses them as a springboard for contemporary fiction in which life and death and past and present intermingle.

'Tydfil' begins with an evocation of the ancient, wooded landscape that would have been the saint's home in the mid-fifth century. Here, portrayed as having run from a proposed marriage to a 'local warlord'[4] and living as a hermit, Tydfil has built herself two small huts by the local river, one as a home for herself and one as her church. Her only company is an occasional visit from Brother Pedr, another hermit living a half day's walk away. Together, they hear each other's confessions and absolve each other.

With the calls and songs of birds and the 'laughter of the river as it trips and hurries over stones towards the sea',[5] it might be easy to think that this idyll is impossible to find in a place that became the scene of huge industrial expansion and mining activity from the late eighteenth century – but if you look you can still discover it by going a couple of miles north to Cwm Taf Fechan.

There, on winding paths in a sylvan landscape, you can walk on either side of the River Taff as it indeed laughs, trips and hurries over stones and boulders, and even goes through a small gorge, on its way south to Cardiff and the Bristol Channel. Nearby, the Taff Trail cycle route makes for an easier route to follow but for the real 'Tydfil' experience the footpaths are a must.[6]

However, with the young woman's life ending when men on horseback come down the valley killing her and burning down her two huts, she remains close by in a something like a ghostly form, observing what happens in the place of her death: Merthyr Tydfil. Somewhat surprised that the significance and location of her little church is remembered she notices, perhaps a century or two after her demise, that it has been rebuilt with a cross beside it. Sometime later she remarks on it again, now reconstructed in stone and even containing an image of her to be reverenced.

Then, hundreds of years pass and Tydfil finds it difficult to locate her church among the many buildings and the very urban environment that now surrounds it. But, once discovered, it's seen to have been rebuilt yet again and 'has become a dark, solemn building'[7] although it is still in the place where she met her death.

Meanwhile, Tydfil listens and responds to the thoughts of young women who come to her church over the centuries to pray and to enjoy the silence in the midst of difficult lives. In her supernatural form, she tries to reassure them of her presence and even to act on their behalf. 'Tydfil' ends with the plight of a homeless, teenage pick-pocket of our own times.

Herrad's story is remarkable on numerous counts but above all it's a re-imagining in literature of the importance of place in the story of Wales and its churches.

Today, St Tydfil's Old Parish Church continues to mark the site of the saint's death,[8] this building being a fine, late Victorian structure which replaced a previous place of worship built earlier in nineteenth century. This, too, was a replacement for the stone-built medieval church which would have succeeded at least one earlier church built of wood and wattle.

However, inside there is an interesting survivor from the early medieval period, this being an inscribed stone which dates to between about 600 and 800. Recognised as significant when it was in place as a building material on the exterior of the Old Parish Church's immediate predecessor, the rebuilding in 1894 allowed for the relocation of this artefact to a safe position where it could be both viewed and studied.

It can only be assumed that this stone was also used as part of the structure of the medieval church, having been discarded when its original purpose as a memorial was no longer seen as important. The stone's vertical inscription *Artbeu* records the name of the person commemorated. As a cross is also inscribed, the wording can then be interpreted as 'Artbeu's cross'.[9] With its history going back to the time when the church would have been a simple wooden structure, there is nothing to suggest that the stone has not been associated with this site since just a century or two after Tydfil's own time.

Meanwhile another ancient stone, although in this case a rather earlier one of the Romano-British period, is displayed alongside the smaller *Artbeu* in the eastern end of the north aisle of the church. With a more sophisticated inscription than its neighbour, which can be translated as *the son of Anniccius, the son of Tecurus. He lies here in this tomb*, the stone is well-documented as having been found at a farm several miles north of Merthyr Tydfil and to have been moved to the parish church in about 1900.

Caldey Island – on the trail of St Samson

OS: SS 143 966

The contemporary statue of Samson on Caldey Island portrays the saint, the patron of Caldey, as a kindly cleric carrying an episcopal staff. The statue is found not far from the Abbey of Our Lady and St Samson which is home to the Cistercian community that is the current owner of the island.

Born in about 485 in the kingdom of Dyfed in south-west Wales, Samson was the child 'of distinguished and noble parents',[10] Amon and Anna. While Amon was local to that area, his wife was a native of Gwent over to the east. Both, however, had fathers who were 'court officials of the kings of their respective provinces'.[11]

A much longed-for son born after years of childlessness, Samson left his childhood home at the age of five to live under the guardianship of St Illtud, 'the famous master of the Britons',[12] at Llantwit Major. There he received his education and training for the monastic life to which he had been dedicated from birth.

With not only his parents but also his uncle and aunt and their children having renounced their worldly goods 'for they were possessed of abundant means',[13] the extended family sought to endow monasteries and churches which would be dedicated by Samson. Meanwhile, the young man, having completed his studies, travelled to the monastery of Abbot Piro on Caldey in search of a more ascetic life than that which he had experienced at Llantwit Major.

However, all does not seem to have been well on Caldey, as Piro was then killed after an accident incurred while under the influence of alcohol. Now without a spiritual leader for their community, the brethren urged Samson to become abbot.

Believed to have held this position for about eighteen months, Samson's life then changed again when 'distinguished Irishmen, on their way from Rome'[14] arrived at the island monastery. Having spent much time in conversation with the visitors and having gained the permission of the bishop, Samson decided to accompany the men on their journey home. This is thought to have been at Dun Etair which is the promontory now known by its Viking name of Howth on the northern extremity of Dublin Bay.[15]

Having very much impressed his hosts with his sanctity and miracle-working powers, as he made preparations for return, Samson was then given the said monastery to which his uncle later returned as abbot.

Once back in south Wales and having spent some time spent in seclusion near the Severn estuary with a few companions, Samson was consecrated a bishop and set off for Cornwall. Here, one of the first places he visited was a monastery at a place called *Docco*, which is believed to have been on the site of what is now the parish church of St James the Great in the village of St Kew. Perhaps a daughter house of Llandough (*Llandochau*) in the Vale of Glamorgan, the mention of *Docco* would seem to support the view that Cornwall was already the object of missionary endeavour from Wales. However, in what can seem a rather amusing incident to us today, the perhaps overly austere Samson is asked to leave by the local abbot on the grounds that the religious life as lived at his monastery is not sufficiently rigorous for the visiting cleric.

Samson then proceeded on his journey to Brittany but not before he had founded a monastery of his own, thought to be either at Golant (*Golnans*) or at South Hill (*Bre Dheghow*), where churches dedicated to Samson exist to this day.[16] And although Golant tends to be favoured as the more likely site, perhaps because it is situated on what is seen as the probable land route taken by travellers from south Wales, the graveyard of the parish church at South Hill contains a remarkable early Christian memorial stone,[17] which just might be the one referred to in the *Life* where the author comments 'on this hill I myself have been and have adored and with my hand have traced the sign of the cross which St Samson with his own hand carved by means of an iron instrument on a standing stone'.[18]

All in all, it would certainly seem reasonable to consider the claim of South Hill to be the place where the saint from Wales established his Cornish monastery and where the anonymous writer tells us that he was given material relating to his subject. The evidence of the church's dedication, the topographical detail of the hill (the east Cornwall hamlet is at an altitude of 166 metres, with the land sloping away particularly to the east and west) and the presence of the sixth-century inscribed stone must surely constitute a strong case. Recent archaeological excavations carried out in the course of drainage works have also provided considerable evidence for early medieval burials in the churchyard. [19]

However, whether taking leave of South Hill or Golant, Samson then continued his journey to the western fringes of the continent of Europe. There he would go on to take his place as one of the founder saints of Brittany, where his *Life* was written about a hundred years after his death. Closely associated with the establishment of a monastery that would evolve into the cathedral at Dol-de Bretagne (*Dol*),[20] Samson is also likely to have been the founder of another religious house at Pental, further to the east near the mouth of the Seine and now in Normandy. His travels between Cornwall and Brittany may also have taken him to Guernsey, where a church is dedicated to him.[21] In addition, he appears to have been in Paris sometime between 556 and 573, where he attended a church council with fellow bishops.

But it is also in the world of scholarship and research that Samson continues to leave a very interesting trail to follow, with his *Life* having been the subject of a colloquy convened as part of the University of Sydney's Conference of Celtic Studies held in June 2013.[22] There, scholars of international standing discussed issues not only relating to the dating of the *Life* (there is now a reasonable consensus that this was written in about 700) and its influence on later Breton hagiography, but also considered the material relating to Samson which the author claimed he had been entrusted with when in Cornwall. Their deliberations included what form this might have taken and what use was made of it in the author's own work: '[the old man] kindly related to me many particulars of the saint's wonderful career',[23] although the existence of an earlier Cornish *Life*, a *Vita Primagenia*, was generally discounted.

Meanwhile, Samson's exploits, and a later ninth-century *Life* which focuses more on the saint's achievements once he had arrived in Brittany, have continued to be followed and studied by academics from around the world.[24]

Surely, this is real international fame for the young man from sixth century west Wales. Rather amusingly perhaps, this group of scholars have taken to themselves the name of 'Samsonites'!

St Mungo on High Street, Glasgow

OS: NS 601 653

St Mungo can be found on a mural trail commissioned by Glasgow City Council, with the aim of this major project being the rejuvenating and revitalising of the streets and buildings of Scotland's biggest urban area.[25]

Completed in 2016 by the Australian-born but now Glasgow-based contemporary street artist Smug,[26] the gigantic figure of Mungo was made using cans of spray paint. The result is an extraordinarily realistic portrait of the saint dressed in the everyday clothes of the twenty-first century. With his woollen beanie-style hat, hoodie and zipped jacket, a middle-aged Mungo looks tenderly at a robin perched on his hand, while another bird flutters just above his shoulder. A few streets away his mother, St Enoch, is portrayed by the same artist as she cradles her infant son in her arms. In a pose suggesting she is breast-feeding the baby, again a robin is included, this time on Enoch's hand close to the infant's back.

Almost all of what we know of Mungo, including a story about a robin, comes from the *Life of Kentigern* written by Jocelin of Furness in about 1180.[27] Here, Jocelin writes how, as a boy, the saint had already been given his alternative name (meaning 'my dear one') by St Servanus, into whose care and tutelage he had been placed. However, other boys also being instructed by the older man grew jealous of the favour Mungo enjoyed and, when a pet robin was killed in a classroom squabble, the young saint was falsely accused of being the one who had caused the little bird to die when its head was severed from its body. But, after placing the lifeless creature in his hand and praying for the robin to be restored, a miracle was instantly granted. With the bird fluttering over to Servanus as he returned from church, Mungo was confirmed as one who was especially blessed by God and who would go on to be exalted by Him.

Jocelin of Furness also describes how, later in his

adult life, Mungo had to leave his native Strathclyde after incurring the dislike of the pagan King Morken, whereupon he fled to Wales to seek safety. There, he not only met St David but was invited to found a religious community by King Cathwalain,[28] eventually deciding on a site that would come to be named, in English, after the young St Asaph who was one of his pupils.

With no other sources available to us to corroborate Jocelin's account of Mungo's sojourn in Wales, his association with Asaph can seem doubtful. However, it's important to remember the shared dynastic and linguistic heritage of the kingdom of Strathclyde and north Wales in the post-Roman period. At the time the Brittonic language that would go on to evolve into Welsh was still spoken in the south of Scotland and Cumbria (where it was later known as Cumbric), while Cunedda, a fifth-century chieftain from what is now the Scottish borders, is believed to have settled in north Wales in order to repel raiding parties from Ireland, and to have been the progenitor of the kings of Gwynedd. Thus, in the wider context of the links between the two regions of Britain, the saint's stay in Wales is quite plausible. In addition, a thirteenth-century charter[29] may well incorporate much earlier stories of how the saint was given land for his new foundation, and he is generally accepted as having established what would much later become the cathedral of St Asaph, although his association with David is unlikely.

Eventually though, following God's vengeance on King Morken for his evil ways, Mungo was able to return to Strathclyde following the accession of the godly and Christian king, Rederech.[30] There, he established a bishopric at Holdelm (now Hoddam in the county of Dumfries and Galloway), although after a few years this was relocated to what is now Glasgow.

Today, the oldest sections that can be observed at St Asaph's Cathedral date from the thirteenth century, and the building is the focal point of the Diocese of St Asaph, one of six such areas in the Church in Wales.

St Tydecho at Llanymawddwy

OS: SH 903 191

I first came across Tydecho at the parish church in Mallwyd, a village in the southernmost part of Gwynedd and just inside Eryri National Park. There, in the entrance area to the building, can be seen an annotated local Ordnance Survey map, together with photos. The work of a former resident, this display indicates several features associated with the saint on a hillside further up the Dyfi Valley.

One of four churches in this area dedicated to Tydecho, Mallwyd is thought to be a later medieval foundation with the now-closed church about six miles away at Llanymawddwy believed to be the site where this sixth-century saint may have established a small religious house or hermitage.[31] Passing through the parish in the early years of the seventeenth century, the antiquary George Owen (c.1552–1613) observed that a decayed, separate chapel was still in existence in the churchyard and that within this structure (which is no longer visible) local people kept a vigil to the saint on Friday evenings.

As with many people associated with the Age of the Saints, there is little in the way of evidence for Tydecho that goes back to the early medieval period, except for the dedication itself and the recording of a sixth-century Latin-incised stone (which was subsequently lost) having been found in the churchyard in 1746. However, late medieval Welsh poetry preserves several traditions as regards the saint and the quite dramatic landscape of this area. It is these that have been taken to reconstruct a simple pilgrimage of exploration for which details can be found at Mallwyd.

With no *Vita* as such known to us, it would appear that Dafydd Llwyd ap Llywelyn ap Gruffudd (c.1420–c.1500) had access to written or aural sources, perhaps including an earlier *Life*, when he wrote his *cywydd*[32] in praise of Tydecho in the mid or later fifteenth century.

Available in English in a translation by the Rev. Griffith Edwards (1812–1893), the poem includes references to the saint's bed and seat, places that can still be found by the determined pilgrim. Of the former, Edwards' words read: 'His bed beneath the mountain's brow, Was the hard rock we see there now.' Meanwhile, a few lines later, 'Maelgwyn the king on mischief bent',[33] is described as sitting on the saint's own seat to observe the miracle, after his theft of Tydecho's cattle, of deer pulling the plough, with a tame wolf assisting. But, trying to get up, Maelgwyn finds that he is stuck by his bottom to the rock as punishment for his misdeeds, only being set free when he has restored the oxen. Meanwhile, Dafydd Llwyd's work is also the source for the tradition that the saint received land at Garthbeibio from 'the wicked Cynon' as restitution following his abduction of Tydecho's sister, Tegfedd.

Another poet, Matthew Brwmffild, whom we know was active between 1520 and 1560, also includes mention of Tydecho in his work. In a poem eulogising the beauty and bounty of both Mallwyd and Llanymawddwy, he alludes to a story of how the saint miraculously caused a stream to turn to milk: 'And the brook running from the height, He turned to milk all pure and white.'[34] To this day the Llaethnant continues to look rather like milk (*llaeth*) as it cascades down the steep hillside to join the little River Rhiwlech (*Afon Rhiwlech*), together forming the infant River Dyfi.[35]

Of course, Brwmffild appears to have been aware of Dafydd Llwyd's earlier work but his inclusion of the story of the stream suggests that he too may also have had access to sources that have since disappeared. However, Tydecho is not without a mention in earlier writings. He appears briefly in the *Life of St Padarn* where he is mentioned as one of a group of Breton saints who have arrived in west Wales by sea. This *Vita* almost certainly incorporated previous material, although it is now thought that Tydecho and the others may have come from a less distant place, perhaps in south-east Wales.

Be that as it may, the traditions surrounding Tydecho certainly highlight the likely significance of the Dyfi, and other rivers flowing west, as a means of access inland to those making their way from Cardigan Bay (*Bae Ceredigion*) and the Irish Sea.

Meanwhile, contemporary travellers and pilgrims can get their instructions at Mallwyd and also make their way up to Llanymawddwy. Here, although the church is no longer in use and includes very little of the medieval fabric, the graveyard includes a venerable ancient yew tree. Known to be one of several still in existence in the nineteenth century, and with a girth at ground level of about nine metres, the yew is to the north-east of the church.[36] And although it is no longer possible to gain access to the building, it contains a distinctive Romanesque font which believed to date to the eleventh century.[37]

From Llanymawddwy, it's about a mile and half north on a minor road to the valley of the Llaethnant, Tydecho's milky stream. Taking a public footpath (SH 905213), this can be followed, quite steeply at times, in a north-west direction; and although the way feels remote, with splendid views of a rugged Aran Fawddwy appearing in the distance, it is all on a very good and clear path. After a while though, the path leads north above the Ceunant y Briddell and becomes more indistinct and, overall, most walkers and pilgrims will be better off making this a there-and-back route.[38]

Returning to the church at Mallwyd, on the north wall of the nave a memorial, with an extensive Latin inscription, can be seen to Dr John Davies, who was rector here for thirty years in the early seventeenth century. The new edition of the Bible, which was published in 1620 (this being a revision of William

Morgan's work of 1588), was undertaken by the very learned Davies.

Another feature, surely unique, are the large whalebones displayed at the entrance to the church. More conventionally, the churchyard is home, as at Llanymawddwy, to an ancient yew tree.[39]

Endnotes

Preface

1   The *Tro-Breiz* is a 700-kilometre-long pilgrimage connecting the seven ancient cathedrals of Brittany and commemorating their origins in the sixth and seventh centuries. See *A Celtic Pilgrimage*, pp. 72–73.

Chapter 1: A town centre car park and the beginnings of the Christian faith in Wales

1   *The Acts of the Apostles*, 28:16–30, describes St Paul's arrival in Rome and the conditions, which might be described as house arrest, under which he was held prisoner.

2   *The Gospel of St Luke*, 2:1, KJV.

3   This issue is discussed in both my previous books. See *A Celtic Pilgrimage*, p. 125, and *A Pilgrimage Around Wales*, p. 117.

4   The fort at Llandovery probably dates from the advance into Wales in the 70s. It is unknown whether it was occupied after the middle of the second century. For more details about the archaeology of the site, see the Roman Military page of the website of the Dyfed Archaeological Trust (*Ymddiriedolaeth Archaeolegol Dyfed*).

5   Information at Castle Car Park, Llandovery, SA20 0AW.

6   The Caerwent bowl, along with many other finds from the Roman town then known as *Venta*, can be seen in the Newport Museum and Art Gallery, John Frost Square, Newport, NP20 1PA. This is one of only two examples of the *chi-rho* symbol (this was a monogram formed from the first two letters of the Greek word for Christ superimposed on each other) found on artefacts relating to the Roman period in Wales. However, it must be said that some goods imported from the area of the Mediterranean may have had the chi-rho symbol stamped on them, rather like a trademark. The Caerwent bowl may be such an example.

7   The historic gold mines at Dolaucothi are now owned by the National Trust and managed as a visitor attraction.

8   For more details of the amphitheatre and the Romans more generally, see 'The Romans in Carmarthenshire' on the Discover Carmarthenshire website.

9   Llan Teulydawc is one of the 'seven bishop houses of Dyfed'
      mentioned in twelfth-century Welsh lawbooks.

10   For discussion of 'an apparent multiplicity of short-lived
      bishoprics' in the border area of south-east Wales and
      Herefordshire, see Petts, p.171.

11   Three of the Penmachno stones were discovered in the mid-
      nineteenth century when the medieval church was demolished,
      with a further stone found built into a wall in the village. The
      fifth was found a few miles away along the course of a Roman
      road. The inscriptions include the phrases: Carausius lies here in
      this heap of stones; Cantiorix a citizen of Gwynedd lies here. He
      was the cousin of Maglus the magistrate; in the time of Justin the
      consul; Oria lies here. For further details of the collection (which
      also includes a twelfth-century grave slab) and the original Latin,
      see site record for St Tudclud's Church, Penmachno on the
      Coflein website.

12   Although the famous instructions from the Emperor Honorius
      (reigned 393–423) that the people of Roman Britain must now
      defend themselves from the tribes invading what had been the
      Empire dates to 410, it is thought that Roman garrisons had
      been withdrawn from Wales by around 390.

13   The Penmachno inscriptions were also expertly worked by
      craftsmen who are thought to have understood what they were
      writing, itself an indication of the persistence of Roman culture.

14   The information provided by Cadw at St Cian's also includes
      a map indicating the sites of other Latin-incised stones in this
      area. Notable among these are the stones now in the church of
      St Hywyn in Aberdaron. See A Pilgrimage Around Wales, p. 114.
      (Cadw is the Wales-wide organisation that works to protect the
      historic environment on behalf of the Welsh government.)

15   Ogham was simple script used to write down early Irish. See A
      Pilgrimage Around Wales, p. 115.

16   See the website We Learn Welsh.

17   'The exact nature of the rights on these routes and the existence
      of any restrictions may be checked with the local highway
      authority.' This is in contrast to the range of routes which are
      'Public rights of way'. See any current Ordnance Survey map in
      the Explorer or Landranger series.

18   For interesting discussion about the origin of this name, see the
      website aslanhub.com.

19   For incomparable information on Roman roads and their
      construction, see the website of The Roman Roads Research
      Association which aims to continue the work of Ivan D.
      Margary (1896–1976) and his gazetteer, Roman Roads of Britain
      (1955). The numbering scheme devised by Margary to denote

Roman roads is similar to that used for modern roads across the UK.

20 Codrington's extensive survey 'Roman Roads in Britain' can be found on the Internet Archive website.

21 This section of Sarn Helen is a few miles to the east and south of what is now Aberystwyth and considerably south of where I met the couple with the Land Rover.

22 One of these churches is at Llanbadarn Fawr (Powys).

Chapter 2: Setting sail

1 They had travelled from their home in Belgium and across France to Brittany and from there taken the ferry to Rosslare in County Wexford. They had then driven to Northern Ireland and sailed from Larne to Stranraer in southern Scotland. They had then travelled through northern England, into north Wales and Snowdonia and, when I met them near Corwen, they were heading for south Wales.

2 When I was walking on the *Tro-Breiz* in Brittany, I lost count of the number of references I saw to Llantwit Major at local sites. However, when outlining the route that I took on pilgrimage around Wales, I have frequently had to explain why I chose the town as one of the key points on my itinerary. See *A Pilgrimage Around Wales*, p. 64.

3 The physical evidence for the port is ten oak timber piles and the line of a stone pier. See Davies, P., and Williams, A.T., 'The Enigma of the Destruction of Colhuw Port, Wales', *Geographical Review*, Vol. 81, No. 3, 1991, pp. 257–266.

4 There has been an ongoing debate as to whether dredging on the Nash Bank just offshore from this section of the Glamorgan coast is the cause of the loss of sand on this and other local beaches. The Nash Bank was deposited in the last Ice Age and has been commercially dredged for sand for use in construction since the 1920s. It should perhaps be noted that there is currently a licence in place to allow dredging of the west end of the bank. The boulders on the beach at Llantwit Major have been placed there to try to reduce the loss of sand.

5 There is a very interesting map in the collection of the British Library showing the coastline of the Severn Estuary between Gloucester and Cardiff in about 1595. The work of an unknown cartographer, the map clearly depicts the tidal inlets on either side of the Severn. Unfortunately, the map stops just short of Llantwit Major but it clearly shows how many potential sheltered anchorages and so on have been lost to silting up, urbanisation, erosion and so on.

6   The Barlands Farm boat was discovered in the course of building
     a supermarket supply depot. Interestingly, it was found about
     two miles inland, alongside the remains of a Roman quay, in
     what was a long-silted up inlet of the Severn estuary. See the
     Living Levels website.

7   This is the sixteenth-century Stradling correspondence noted
     by Davies and Williams (see endnote 3). Another interesting
     discussion as regards the considerable number of ports in
     the Bristol Channel area, admittedly also in the Tudor era, is
     *The Maritime Trade of the Smaller Bristol Channel Ports in the
     Sixteenth Century* (2009) by Duncan Taylor. This Ph.D. thesis
     challenges the perceived dominance of the port of Bristol
     and includes considerable documentation of ports such as
     Bridgwater, including its trade in Welsh iron. I think it would be
     reasonable to assume that places such as Bridgwater and nearby
     Minehead in Somerset and Barnstable in Devon were already
     developing as anchorages in the early medieval period.

8   My route that year was determined by the ferry crossing from
     Plymouth to Roscoff in Brittany. However, the time I had
     committed to this project allowed me to walk west of Plymouth
     and on to Fowey and as far as Truro. See *A Celtic Pilgrimage*, p.
     16.

9   The identity of St Fimbarrus is very uncertain. He may be the
     same person as St Finnbar (*c.*550–623), the first bishop of Cork
     in the south of Ireland, who is thought to have travelled across
     Cornwall to Brittany on several occasions. Fimbarrus is a useful
     reminder of the importance of Cornwall to those on journeys
     from Ireland as well as from Wales. Alternatively, the church's
     dedication may be to a local saint, Barry, a possible associate of
     another Cornish saint, Neot, whose feast day he shares. See the
     Britain Express website for more discussion on the identity of St
     Fimbarrus.

10   The Saints' Way is overseen by Cornwall County Council.

11   Just a few hundred metres off the route to Polkerris on the
     Saints' Way is the Tristan Stone, situated alongside the
     B3415 just outside Fowey. Inscribed with sixth-century Latin
     DRUSTANS HIC IACET CUNOMORI FILIUS (Here lies
     Drustanus, the son of Cunomorus), the stone is thought to
     commemorate the original Tristan whose doomed love for Isolt
     inspired many later interpretations of their story. Although the
     belief that the stone refers to Tristan has been challenged, 'There
     is little reason to doubt that the stone belongs to the historic
     Tristan'. Davies (1997), p. 223. For more discussion of the stone
     and the local context, see the page The Tristan Stone on the
     Cornwall Guide website.

12   I was to revisit the Saints' Way on a later pilgrimage to St
      Michael's Mount, walking the section between Golant and
      Padstow.

13   Although generally still referred to as a cathedral, the building's
      status since the early nineteenth century is that of a church
      following the reduction of the number of dioceses in Brittany
      from its pre-Revolution number of nine to five in 1801. In 1852
      the diocese into which it had been subsumed was renamed 'The
      Diocese of Saint-Brieuc and Tréguier'.

14   The other side of the tomb shows the funeral rites of Sainte-
      Pompée with Tugdual and two monks, together with a
      crucifixion scene.

15   Writing in the thirteenth century, the scholar Albert of Cologne
      described how Tugdual received gifts of land from the great
      landowners to whom he preached. At one of these a religious
      house, headed by Sève, was founded. Nothing remains of
      this convent but the modern village of Sainte-Sève (Sant Seo)
      perpetuates her name.

16   Notably, the founder saints include St Samson of Dol, about
      whom we probably know the most and who is discussed in
      chapter 12, and Paul Aurelian (known in France as St Pol de
      Léon) who appear to have the strongest links with what is now
      Wales. Like Samson, Paul Aurelian is believed to have studied
      at Llantwit Major. St Malo, known by many variants of his
      name and with what seems to be quite a confused history, also
      appears to be associated with Llancarfan in Glamorgan. One
      probable exception among them as regards coming from Wales
      is St Corentin, the putative founder of the cathedral at Quimper,
      who seems to have been born in Brittany to parents who had
      emigrated from Britain. However, it must be said, as regards
      Padarn, another of the seven founder saints and, by tradition, the
      same person as the founder of Llanbadarn Fawr in Ceredigion,
      that this is now considered to perhaps be a case where two men
      of the same (common) name have been confused. Meanwhile, it
      has been proposed that St Brieuc originated in Ireland but went
      to Brittany via Wales and western Britain.

17   With Gaul having been conquered by Julius Caesar by 50 BCE,
      the province of Gallia Lugdenensis, centred on Lyon, was created
      in 22 BCE when Gaul was sub-divided into three.

18   There was also some settlement by Romano-Britons in the late
      fifth and early sixth centuries to an area of north-west Spain
      (then part of the Germanic kingdom of the Suebi) which became
      known as Britonia. In contrast to settlements in Brittany, those
      on the Iberian peninsula soon lost their linguistic distinctiveness.
      In recent times, there have been moves in what is now the

Spanish province of Galicia for the area to be considered one of
the family of Celtic nations. However, these have been resisted
by some on linguistic grounds on the basis of what could be
identified as a Celtic language appearing to have died out
there by the ninth century. See an interesting blog by Emmett
McIntyre, dated 11 December 2013, on the Transceltic website.

19   It is unclear just what language was being used by ordinary
people in this area of Brittany at this time, with the relationship
between Gaulish (the Celtic language of what is now France and
other areas of Western Europe) and what is known as Vulgar
Latin being uncertain. However, it is thought that Gaulish and
Latin were still co-existing in the sixth century, with Gregory
of Tours (c.538–594) being witness to this. Meanwhile, the
relative influences of Brittonic and Gaulish on the evolution of
Breton remain a topic of debate with the Breton scholar, Léon
Fleuriot, (1923–1987), proposing a model in which the former
predominated. An opposing, and generally minority view,
in favour of Breton being mainly dependent on Gaulish was
championed by fellow academic, François Falc'hun (1901–1991).
Also see my own comments about discussing Breton with a
native speaker, *A Celtic Pilgrimage*, pp.76–7.

20   It should be noted how few Roman roads and settlements there
were in much of Brittany. However, the site of one Roman fort at
Le Yaudet, near Lannion, is also associated with an early Roman
bishopric. See *A Celtic Pilgrimage*, p. 86. Although St Martin of
Tours (316–397) attempted the consolidation of the new faith
in the later Roman period, it would appear that the Diocese of
Tours had only nominal control over Brittany in Tugdual's time.
Moreover, it's hard not to draw the conclusion that, as with west
Wales and Cornwall, the Roman occupation of Brittany was only
slight.

21   For the three *Vitae* of Tugdual (in Latin but also translated into
French and with extensive notes and analysis), see Arthur de La
Borderie, *Histoire de Bretagne, Critique des sources* (Paris, 1887),
which is available online at Google Books. Arthur Le Moyne de
La Borderie (1827–1901) is considered to be the father of the
historiography of Brittany and someone whose scholarship one
can only be in awe of. His discussion of the usefulness of the
Anglo-Saxon Chronicle in dating Tugdual's arrival in Brittany to
between 520 and 530 is of particular interest. For this, see pp.
58–59. More recently, the historian Bernard Tanguy (1940–2015)
has re- evaluated the medieval record as to Tugdual. It must also
be said that academic study of (Latin) texts in relation to the
saint is almost exclusively in French.

22   St Tudwal's Island East (*Ynys Tudwal Fach*) is thought to have

been home to a community of Augustinian Canons from the late thirteenth century, although it remains unclear if it was preceded by an early medieval religious community on the same site. For discussion of Augustinian houses on previous early medieval sites, see chapter 5.

Chapter 3: On a tiny island and excursions to the Wirral and the Isle of Man

1   The other island churches are the ruined St Dwynwen's Church on Llanddwyn Island (*Ynys Llanddwyn*) and the still active St Cwyfan's Church on the island of Cribinau near Aberffraw, with both of these being tidal islands. There are also the remains of a monastic settlement on Puffin Island (*Ynys Seiriol*) off the east coast of Anglesey.

2   The Menai Suspension Bridge was completed in 1826, being the first bridge to connect Anglesey with the mainland of north Wales. It is a Grade I-listed structure, being built as part of the improvement of communications between London and Holyhead, and from there by ferry to Ireland.

3   'In 1914 a group of refugees from Mechelen, Belgium, were driven from their home town by the German invasion and found asylum in Menai Bridge.' Information at site.

4   These maps can be viewed on the very useful Anglesey Maps website, where it can also be seen that on Emanuel Bowen's map of 1720 the causeway appears to come on to Church Island from a north-northwest direction. The modern OS map also indicates the remains of a structure below the high tide mark, in a position close to the causeway, as on the Bowen map.

5   *Canu Tysilio*, 'an ode of praise to St Tysilio', edited by Ann Parry Owen, can be read in English and also in Welsh on the Seintiau website.

6   The village of St-Suliac (*Sant-Suliav*), situated near the mouth of the River Rance and south of St-Malo, is on the route of the *Tro-Breiz* pilgrimage.

7   'Tyssilio was the son of Brochwel Ysgythrog, son of Cyngen, son of Cadell Deyrnllwg; and Arddun, daughter of Pabo Post Prydain of the north, was his mother.' See p. 595 in the *Lives of the Cambro British Saints* by the Rev. W.J. Rees, which is available on the Internet Archive website. Various genealogies of the saints (*Achau y Saint*) exist in documents surviving from as early as the twelfth century although they are very likely to include material which is much older. Often attached to saints' lives, two were included in the Rev. W.J. Rees' volume.

8   Examples would include the Rev. Elias Owen MA FSA, in his

essay on circular churchyards published in 1897, 'The many circular churchyards in Wales must have thus been formed designedly, and it is difficult not to associate these round churchyards with the remains of pre-historic times of similar form.'

9   A map from 1913, including what was then the village of Woodchurch, shows that any curvilinearity on the west side of the churchyard had already been lost by 1913. However, when compared with the current Ordnance Survey map, it is interesting to see how several of the pre-1914 roads and boundaries around the church remain today.

10   The place-name Landican combines the Llan/Lan prefix with what may have been the name of an early saint, Tegan or Tecwyn. In the Domesday Book, the name was recorded in Norman French as *Landechesne*. Apart from the name, there is no record of any church having been on the site of Landican itself, so it would appear that Woodchurch and Landican were conflated, with the Norman name (meaning church of oak or wood) seeming to verify this. This may also perhaps be a case of the original place of the saint's 'lan' being superseded by the site of Woodchurch later in the Anglo-Saxon period. The arrival of Anglo-Saxons on the Wirral from the late seventh century (as evidenced in their place-names) and also the discovery of a wheel-headed cross, probably from the tenth century, at Woodchurch seem to support the case that Landican is a very early, now lost, church site which was superseded by Woodchurch. An alternative view, that Landican derives from Lan-diacon, 'church of the deacon', seems unconvincing. Also on the Wirral, it should be noted as well that the parish church at Bromborough has what is believed to be an early medieval curvilinear graveyard (which contains a similar but more complete tenth-century cross to that at Woodchurch) and that the site of a now demolished medieval church at Upton also preserves an early near-circular enclosure.

11   For further discussion of Lancaut, Gloucestershire, see chapter 10 and the section Picturesque Piercefield, Tintern and Lancaut.

12   This issue is discussed very cogently by Dr Edith Evans in her report, *Early medieval ecclesiastical sites in southeast Wales* (2003), where her findings could certainly be considered to apply to a wider area than the examples dealt with in this survey. Also see my own comments on this is issue in *A Celtic Pilgrimage*, p. 134.

13   Evans gives the interesting example of Newchurch in Monmouthshire, where it is known that a church was established on what had been a wooded site in the Wentwood

area of south Wales in the early twelfth century. Curved banks discernible in the now rectilinear churchyard are evidence for a curvilinear enclosure around a Norman church. Evans, p. 27.

14 The churchyard at Nantmel in Powys is an example of what appears to be a double enclosure, with an almost complete curvilinear outer enclosure but, also, to the north and south of the church of St Cynllo, earthen banks which appear to be the remains of an earlier, smaller enclosure.

15 St Peter's has some notable late Anglo-Saxon stonework, although the inner enclosure almost certainly precedes this by several centuries. See *A Guide to St Peter's Church, Stanton Lacy* by Peter Klein (1989).

16 Jocelin of Furness was active between 1175 and 1214. He was a Cistercian monk at Furness Abbey, now in Cumbria in the north of England, and a notable medieval hagiographer. The very picturesque ruins of Furness Abbey are now in the care of English Heritage.

17 Jocelin of Furness' *Life of Patrick* is available on the Internet Archive website in a translation by James O'Leary, published in 1904. The section about Maughold is on pp.298–301.

18 Muirchu's *Life of St Patrick* is available in English, in White, Newport J.D., *St. Patrick: His Writings and Life* (London 1920).

19 For details and photographs, see the Kirk Maughold section of the Isle of Man Guide website.

20 Kermode's records of his excavations can be found in *The Manx Archaeological Survey*, Fourth Report, 1915, The Manx Natural History and Antiquarian Society. I am grateful to Dave Martin, President of the Isle of Man Natural History and Antiquarian Society, for all his help in accessing various papers relevant to Kirk Maughold including, notably, Megaw, B.R.S., 'The Monastery of St. Maughold', in *Proceedings of the Isle of Man Natural History and Antiquarian Society*, 5, 1950, pp.169–180.

21 *A Short Account of Kirk Maughold in the Diocese of Sodor and Man*, written in 1935 by F.M. Lascelles, gives an interesting description. In it Lascelles makes the claim, which I have not been able to verify, that the church is built on the site of not one but two *keeills*.

22 The similar evolution of early monasteries in relation to Norman settlement in Wales is explored in chapter 6.

23 This was previously at the entrance to the churchyard. Later medieval churchyard crosses are discussed further in chapter 6.

Chapter 4: For the price of my best horse

1   The other bells were found in the villages of Llanarmon,
    Llangwnadl, Llangystenin and Llanrhyddlad (*Llan-Rhûddlad*).

2   A reconstruction of the Llangenny bell was the subject of an
    experiment by Tim Young, a specialist in archaeometallurgy, at
    the National Museum of Wales in 2009. The experiment can be
    viewed online on the Amgueddfa Cymru website.

3   Both iron (without brazing) and copper alloy brazed bells also
    survive from Anglo-Saxon England, notably one of the latter
    found at Marden in Herefordshire, not far from the border with
    Wales. However, the greater range in size and variety of sites
    where they have been discovered makes their association with
    Christian ritual unclear, although it has been proposed that
    those with a copper alloy braze are more closely linked with
    the sites of churches and monasteries and could be associated
    with Irish missions in the north of England. See Hugh Willmott
    & Adam Daubney (2019), 'Of saints, sows or smiths? Copper-
    brazed iron handbells in Early Medieval England'.

4   The finding of the bell perhaps might encourage speculation
    that other early medieval bells could still be discovered. The
    Llangenny bell is also a comparatively recent discovery, being
    found buried in 1790 when the ruins of an early chapel, which
    is thought to have been on the original site of the local church,
    were demolished.

5   The outlaws appear to have been based at nearby Ysbyty
    Ifan. There, the church and hospice built around 1190 by the
    Hospitaller Knights of St John of Jerusalem seem to have been
    taken over by lawless elements. See information at site, St John's
    Church, Ysbyty Ifan.

6   Cormac Bourke, 'Early Ecclesiastical Hand-Bells in Britain and
    Ireland', *The Journal of the Antique Metalware Society*, Volume
    16, June 2008, p.26.

7   Paul Stevens, 'For whom the bell tolls: the monastic site at
    Clonfad 3, Co. Westmeath', which is available on the Academia
    website.

8   See Davies, p. 49, as regards the evidence for non-agricultural
    production in Wales including smithing and the forging of bells.

9   See 'Early Breton Hand-bells revisited' by Cormac Burke, which
    is available on the Academia website.

10 For extensive discussion of the process of digitalisation, see
    Endres, William, 'More than Meets the Eye: Going 3D with an
    Early Medieval Manuscript', in Clare Mills, Michael Pidd and
    Esther Ward, *Proceedings of the Digital Humanities Congress
    2012*, Studies in the Digital Humanities, Sheffield, The Digital
    Humanities Institute, 2014.

11   For more details of the visitor centre and the digitalisation project, see llandeilofawr.org.uk

12   Of the 236 surviving pages, sometimes referred to by the more technical term *folios*, eight are illuminated and on a further four the text is contained within a decorative border.

13   A later medieval inventory of the cathedral library at Lichfield implies that the Gospels were in two volumes. However, with the looting of the library during the English Civil War, these went missing but eventually came into the possession of Frances, Duchess of Somerset, who returned them to the cathedral later in the seventeenth century. It appears to be at this point that the second volume was lost.

14   The Gospel Book has been dated to about 730. This would place it slightly earlier than the *Book of Kells* and just after the *Lindisfarne Gospels*. It should be noted in reference to endnote 15 that both of these have always been in one volume.

15   *pro illo equm optimum... sancti Teiaui super altare*, for his best horse... on the altar of holy Teilo.

16   Getting their name because of their similarity to oriental carpets, carpet pages are a feature of illuminated manuscripts. They include geometric designs, often around the Christian symbol of the cross. Also, Aberlady, now in Lothian, was part of the Kingdom of Northumbria in the eighth century. With Northumbria's links to Iona and also to Ireland, it also been suggested that the Gospel Book could have originated in either of those two places. Details of the Aberlady cross shaft can be found on the Canmore website.

17   The Staffordshire Hoard, discovered near Lichfield in 2009, is the largest collection of Anglo-Saxon gold and silver treasure ever found.

18   For further information on the Lichfield Angel, see the website of Lichfield Cathedral.

19   For extensive discussion on the Hereford Gospels and their provenance, 'most compatible with an origin in Wales', see Gameson, R., 'The insular gospel book at Hereford Cathedral' (2002). This is available online on the Persée website.

20   See the Lichfield Live website.

21   Llancarfan, in the Vale of Glamorgan, is believed to be the site of a monastery founded by Cadoc in the sixth century. The medieval church also contains extensive fifteenth-century wall-paintings which have recently been restored. Meanwhile, Brecon Cathedral, now the seat of the bishops of the Diocese of Swansea and Brecon (*Esgobaeth Abertawe ac Aberhonddu*), was the Benedictine Priory of St John before the Reformation. Hay-on-Wye is the home of the acclaimed and now international Hay Festival (*Gŵyl y Gelli*) of literature.

22 For discussion of this technique and an example of a socket stone in the Whithorn Priory Museum, Scotland, see the website of Historic Environment Scotland.

23 The Margam Stones Museum, to be found on the edge of the churchyard of what is now the parish church (but was formerly the nave of the Cistercian abbey) is in the care of Cadw.

24 One of the remarkable features of the cross of Conbelin is the depiction on it of a monk carrying a satchel-type bag, presumably for the safe carrying of a book.

25 Information at site provided by Cadw. This is in the shelter which houses the church's collection of ancient stones.

Chapter 5: A new order?

1 Dyfrig (*Dubricius c.*450–540) was an early bishop in Morgannwg, but also very much associated with Herefordshire. He is one of several saints to which Llandaff Cathedral (*Eglwys Gadeiriol Llandaf*) is dedicated. Following the building of the first Norman cathedral under Bishop Urban, Dyfrig's remains were removed from Bardsey to Llandaff. Deiniol is thought to have died in 572 and to have been the founder of Bangor Cathedral (*Cadeirlan Bangor*).

2 Chris Potter is also the author of the official guide to this route. See the website of the North Wales Pilgrim's Way. Another more southerly pilgrimage route, St Cadfan's Way, which approaches Bardsey from Tywyn, has recently been developed under the auspices of the Diocese of Bangor.

3 For photographs of St Engan's Church, including discussion of furnishings that may have originated on Bardsey, see the website of the Bro Enlli Ministry Area.

4 English-type names seem to predominate (at least among the abbots) until the mid-fourteenth century, followed by various Welsh names. See the website of Monastic Wales.

5 Apart from early medieval burials discovered nearby, there are no known archaeological remains for the earlier monastery apart from an incised stone, probably a cross slab, dated to the tenth to eleventh centuries. This is now in the Wesleyan Chapel situated close to the tower. It would appear that the buildings associated with both the earlier monastery and the later abbey evolved over time and occupied approximately the same site.

6 The *Céli Dé* or *Culdees*, the 'servants of God', appear to have originated as a movement for monastic reform in eighth-century Ireland. Gerald of Wales also records the monasteries at Beddgelert (also in Gwynedd) and Penmon on Anglesey as being of *Céli Dé*. Both these houses would also go on to become

Augustinian abbeys. For further information on the Augustinian Canons in Wales, see the website Monastic Wales.

7 The ruins of Haughmond Abbey are in the care of English Heritage. I was able to visit this picturesque place as I walked home following my pilgrimage to the Isle of Man.

8 See *A Pilgrimage Around Wales*, p. 122.

9 For a very useful explanation of terms such as 'canons regular' and 'canons secular' and the evolution of the role of stipendiary parish clergy, see the website British History Online.

10 *St Padarn's Church, Llanbadarn Fawr, A Souvenir History.* Available at site.

11 The first two of these old stones are almost certainly corbels from the Romanesque church and would have been among many in a corbel table around the exterior of the church. For further discussion of the possible Sheela Na Gig see the page on Llanbadarn Fawr on the website of the Sheela Na Gig Project.

12 The inscription reads 'VAL FlAVINI'. The stone is thought to have come from Roman Fort of Castell Collen about three miles away. It is presumed that the stone was included in the building material of the earlier church.

13 Only one manuscript survives of the *Vita Sancti Paterni*, this being a copy made in about 1200.

14 For a detailed discussion of the two figures and the possible tensions between Norman and Welsh clerics, see Rita Wood's paper, *The Romanesque Doorway at St Padarn's Church, Llanbadarn Fawr, Radnorshire*. This is available online at the website of the Archaeology Data Service. Rita Wood's paper includes excellent photos and also a reproduction of Stephen W. Williams' drawing of the doorway before the Victorian restoration.

15 A tympanum that is especially similar to the one at Llanbadarn Fawr is to be found at the parish church at Dinton in Buckinghamshire, a place that I was able to visit when I walked on pilgrimage to St Albans. See Wood, p. 55.

16 See the online Dictionary of Welsh Biography. Tremeirchion and its healing cross ('long since demolished') also feature in *A Topographical Dictionary of Wales* published by Samuel Lewis in London in 1849.

17 For an interesting contemporary view, in the form of a poem, on the destruction (albeit often partial), of churchyard crosses, see the review by Dr Nicholas McDowell of Julie Spraggon's book *Puritan Iconoclasm in the English Civil War*. This can be found online on the Reviews in History website.

18 Thomas Pennant's *Tours in Wales* also includes mention of the tomb of David ap Roderic ap Madoc 'prophet and poet' and a

former incumbent at Tremeirchion, who translated the Psalms into Welsh verse.

19   Hopkins was resident at St Beuno's from 1874 to 1877, with some of his greatest poetry, including his masterpiece 'The Wreck of the Deutschland', being written at this time.

20   The retreat centre, formerly the college, is dedicated to St Beuno, a saint of north Wales, who was active in the early seventh century. See *A Pilgrimage Around Wales*, p. 57.

Chapter 6: Pilgrimage in Wales

1   St Winefride's Well Shrine has remained in Roman Catholic guardianship.

2   See *A Pilgrimage Around Wales*, pp. 55–57.

3   The Pembrokeshire Coast National Park was inaugurated in 1952.

4   St Davids Cathedral continues to support and encourage pilgrimage in many ways. See the section on pilgrimage on the cathedral's website.

5   This feature is on a public footpath which seems to have been more of a thoroughfare in the past. It can be difficult to spot, but is just a few hundred metres from the church, the map reference being 080041.

6   See Dyfed Archaeological Trust's (*Ymddiriedolaeth Archaeolegol Dyfed*) *Later Medieval and Early Post-Medieval Threat Related Assessment Work, 2012: Monasteries*, p. 20 and p. 22, for details of St Mary's Hospice, Spittal, and the Whitewell Hospice respectively.

7   Llawhaden Castle is now a free to visit site owned by Cadw.

8   Thomas Compton's painting of the view looking north from Bwlch y Groes in 1818 gives some idea of the grandeur of the scenery, although his viewpoint was just beyond where the cross is situated. The painting can be seen online on the website of People's Collection Wales.

9   At 545 metres this is slightly lower than the highest point on a public road in Wales, this being at the Gospel Pass (*Bwlch yr Efengyl*) near Hay-on-Wye in mid Wales.

10   Ogilby's *Brittania* can be viewed online in the maps section of the fulltable.com website. The route between Holywell and St Davids is shown on slides 66 and 67, with Bwlch y Groes (written as *Bullagroys* in Ogilby's Anglicized spelling) shown on the latter slide on the third column from the left. Llanymawddwy can also be seen at the top of the second column on the same slide, with Mallwyd just below. These are discussed further in chapter 12.

11   A summary of Robert of Shrewsbury's work, including

quotations in English, is included in Hugh Owen's *A history of Shrewsbury* which was published in 1825. This is available online on the Internet Archive website. See p. 37 in this text for the brothers' lament about their lack of relics. Hugh Owen is also the authority (see p. 73) for the stone now forming part of the present reconstructed shrine being in the archdeacon's garden in his own time and that it had previously been built into a bridge following the destruction of the fourteenth century shrine at the Reformation. Owen believed that the shrine's original site had been a chantry chapel in the north aisle, where the present one is now situated.

12 It is thought that whatever remained of Winefride's shrine at Gwytherin may have been destroyed when the medieval church was demolished in 1867. See 'A Fragment of a Reliquary Casket from Gwytherin, North Wales' | The Antiquaries Journal | Cambridge Core (The rebuilt Victorian church is now in private ownership.)

13 In 2016 the 600th anniversary of Henry V's pilgrimage was commemorated in an ecumenical event organised by the Diocese of Shrewsbury.

Chapter 7: Zealots and vandals?

1 The soundscapes that accompany this exhibition, which can be accessed online on the artist's website, are also very thought-provoking.

2 Rood screens are discussed in detail in *A Pilgrimage around Wales*, pp. 69–72.

3 'She hath broken down the lofts that were builded for idolatry.' Words in praise of Queen Elizabeth I from a sermon delivered by Edwins Sandys, Archbishop of York from 1576 to 1588, on the occasion of a royal visit. Williams, p. 95.

4 As can be seen from my photo taken at St Swithun's, the rood loft stairs are inside the north wall of the nave and running straight and parallel to it. The arrangement was the same at Llandefalle and also at St Davids (see note below), and seems to have generally been the case, although occasionally the staircase was of a spiral design. St Swithun's Church is in the care of the Churches Conservation Trust.

5 In most parish churches such as at Llandefalle, there was a single staircase leading to the rood loft, but in larger and more grand churches there seems to often have been a pair of staircases on either side of the loft, allowing for a one-way system for a presumably large number of pilgrims. This arrangement can clearly be seen at the cathedral in Brecon.

6   It is thought that the original dedication may have been to
     St Maelog, with this being lost as a result of Normanisation.
     See *The Church of St Matthew, Llandefalle* by the Rev. Ian
     Charlesworth (2020), adapted and abridged by Mr Chris Taylor.
     Available at site.

7   The only study I am aware of which deals with the proportion of
     churches where the rood loft stairs are still in place is in relation
     to medieval churches of Suffolk where it is thought that about
     half of the county's medieval churches retain this feature.

8   I would have to admit that I also considered climbing the loft
     stairs when I visited St David's, making this the third church
     where this was at least a possibility. However, the building
     was undergoing extensive renovations at the time and the
     stairwell (which here is built into the south wall) was, quite
     understandably, being used for storage.

9   The text on the memorial echoes the words of this verse in
     the Douai Bible published in Reims in 1582. This translation
     of the New Testament (the Old Testament was published in
     the seventeenth century) was made by scholars at the English
     College established at Douai in 1568. In an area that is now close
     to the border with Belgium, the college was founded to train
     men for the Roman Catholic priesthood, with the intention that
     they would return to serve in Wales and England. The Douai
     Bible was a translation of the Vulgate, which was adopted by
     the Roman Catholic Church as its authoritative version in the
     Middle Ages, with this continuing to be the case.

10   An 'Act against Jesuits, seminary priests and other such like
     disobedient persons' was passed in 1584, re-enforcing the Act
     of Supremacy from the start of the reign of Elizabeth I in 1558.
     Members of the then recently instituted Society of Jesus (the
     order received Papal recognition in 1540) were often the target
     of the authorities in Elizabethan England.

11   A digitalised copy of this book can be found on the website of the
     National Library of Wales (*Llyfrgelll Genedlaethol Cymru*).

12   The uplands of Mynydd Epynt are well-known for having been
     requisitioned by the Ministry of Defence in 1940; they continue
     to be a military training area. See Epynt: A lost community -
     NFU Cymru (nfu-cymru.org.uk) However, it is possible to walk
     around the perimeter. See Epynt Way maps - GOV.UK (www.
     gov.uk)

13   Occupying the site of a former Dominican Priory, what is now
     Christ College Brecon was established in 1541.

14   Jesus College, Oxford, was founded in 1571 and soon became
     the favoured institution for a considerable proportion of the
     very small number of young men in Wales who had access to

higher education. Also, although mainly relating to eighteenth-century Montgomeryshire, for a brief but interesting analysis of preferences in choice of university in Tudor Wales, see the opening page of Smith, Douglas W., *Berriew and Trinity: Thomas Jones (1756–1807) and his Contemporaries*. This is available online in the Welsh Journals section of the website of the National Library of Wales.

15   *The Aequity of an Humble Supplication* was published in Oxford in 1587.

16   The considerable historiography associated with Penry is discussed by James Ashdown, a former lay reader at St Cadmarch's Church, on his website which can be found at www.storyman.org.uk. James Ashdown is also the author of *Morwen's Angel – An ancient Celtic story from the Cambrian mountains and a pilgrimage through its beautiful landscape*, which is available at the church.

17   For a transcript of a lecture, 'John Penry: the Early Brecknockshire Puritan Firebrand', delivered by Professor J. Gwynfor Jones, see the website of the Brecknock Society.

18   For a photo of the cross fragment at St Cadmarch's Church, see the website of the Llangammarch Wells History Society.

Chapter 8: A life to live

1   Nonconformity, in a religious sense, is a term that is rooted in the creation, in the sixteenth century, of the Church of England as a state-sanctioned church with the monarch as Supreme Head. From then on, all Anglican clergy had to swear allegiance to the king or queen of the day and also the tenets of the new church. Although the phrase is generally associated with later Protestant dissent, in practice, a wide range of clergy were unable to *conform*, including Roman Catholics.

2   Information at the site.

3   Broadmead Baptist Church, founded in 1640, was the first separatist congregation in the city of Bristol. One of the early members, Edward Terrill (1634–1686), wrote a diary about the opposition faced by the group. This was continued by others and forms the Broadmead Records, which is a valuable primary source for this period and is in the care of Bristol Archives.

4   The full title of this legislation was the 'Act for the Better Propagation of the Preaching of the Gospel in Wales'. Thomas Vaughan was removed from his living at Llansantffraed, near Talybont-on-Usk, under the terms of this Act.

5   St Woolos' Church is now Newport Cathedral (*Cadeirlan Casnewydd*).

6   This is the Brinore Tramroad which is now a signed walking
    trail.

7   A leaflet giving details of the Vaughan Walk is available on the
    Talybont-on-Usk village website. Also, as far as I am aware,
    Talybont-on-Usk is unique in producing its own local colouring
    book, which includes a page featuring Henry Vaughan. The
    colouring book can be purchased from Talybont Stores in the
    centre of the village.

8   This group of poets included George Herbert (1593–1633), who
    was a great influence on Henry Vaughan and to whom he was
    distantly related.

9   The Caerfanell rises in the *Bannau Brycheiniog* to the west of
    Talybont and joins the Usk near the Vaughan's childhood home.
    Its higher reaches are marked by considerable waterfalls before
    the river's course is interrupted by the Talybont Reservoir
    (*Cronfa Ddŵr Tal-y-bont*), which was created in the 1930s.

10 These lines are from Thomas Vaughan's poem 'So I have Spent
    on the Banks of Isca Many a Serious Hour'. This is available
    online on the Poetry Nook website.

11 Taken from 'The Resolve', a poem which was included in *Silex
    Scintillans*, published by Vaughan in 1650.

12 For Sassoon's poem in full, see the Poetry Nook website.

13 The earliest recorded burial at The Pales was in 1683, although it
    would seem likely that there were other unrecorded interments
    after the establishment of the burial ground in 1672, and
    perhaps even before the formalising of the site that year. It has
    been estimated that there were at least 264 burials between 1683
    and 2014, with some of the earliest graves possibly being under
    the meeting house and warden's cottage.

14 Gwynne Stock 'An Evaluation of Quaker Burial Practices'
    (Bournemouth University in collaboration with Bristol and
    Frenchay Monthly Meeting: Unpublished Postgraduate Research
    Diploma, 1997) See 'Summary' prepared by Rebecca Wynter
    (2012), which can be found at Gwynne_Stock.pdf (woodbrooke.
    org.uk)

15 Unfortunately, due to the very simple nature of Quaker 'gardens',
    some have all but disappeared. However, at Quakers Yard, south
    of Merthyr Tydfil, a burial ground can still be found within
    a walled enclosure. Today, this is rather tucked away but a
    photo of the area taken in 1897 clearly shows the site alongside
    the River Taff (*Afon Tâf*). The photo can be found on the Old
    Merthyr Tydfil website in the section on Quakers Yard.

16 John Wildman is thought to be the author of the Leveller
    manifesto, *An Agreement of the People*, which called, among
    various radical proposals, for a single elected House in which

sovereignty would reside. It was re-issued in various editions between 1647 and 1649.

17   Clarke was secretary to the Council of the Army from 1647 to 1649. An edited edition of his transcripts can be found online at 'Puritanism and liberty: Great Britain' on the Internet Archive website.

18   Walter Cradock had been Erbery's curate in Cardiff but he appears to have been dismissed from his Anglican orders by the Bishop of Llandaff in 1634.

19   'John's Spirit in the North of England and the Spirit of Jesus rising in north-Wales, is for the fall of all the Church in the South', *The Testimony of William Erbery*, London (1658).

20   This organisation was closed down in 2022.

Chapter 9: A double grandeur

1   A digitalised facsimile at Gilpin's travelogue can be found on the Internet Archive website.

2   Gilpin, p. 39.

3   Ibid., p. 45.

4   A notable example is his *Llanstephan Castle by Moonlight, with a Kiln in the Foreground*, 1795–96. Also, *Limekiln at Coalbrookdale*, completed in about 1797, featured the processes going on close to the border with Wales near Ironbridge in Shropshire.

5   Thought to have been an early work of the architect Sir John Soane (1753–1837), the house at Piercefield, which includes some remnants of the Walters' Tudor mansion, has been derelict for some time. For details of the house, in the context of its coming onto the market in 2005, see the article 'Sloane's Forgotten Masterpiece' on the website of *Country Life* magazine.

6   For the very interesting guide to the walk, see Layout 1 (visitdeanwye.co.uk)

7   For discussion of the Cistercian houses in Wales, see *A Pilgrimage around Wales*, pp. 125–127.

8   See https://www.tinternvillage.co.uk/whattoseeanddo/ MarianWay/

9   The Wye Valley Walk is a long-distance recreational trail between Plynlimon (*Pumlumon*), the source of the Wye, and Chepstow where it meets the estuary of the Severn.

10   William Wordsworth's poem 'Tintern Abbey' is well-known, but for the poem 'Poetical Description of Tintern Abbey' (1804) by the Chepstow-born poet Edward Davies, see the Tintern village website.

11   Gilpin, p. 55.

12   For very scenic photos of Lancaut, see Anne Griffiths' website Hills, mountains and more.

13   The *Book of Llandaff* (the *Liber Landavensis*) was a compilation
      of various documents made to further the interests of the
      Diocese of Llandaff, particularly in regards to the rival claims of
      the Diocese of Hereford. Included in it are numerous charters,
      some of which date back to the sixth century, which record gifts
      of land which the Diocese laid claim to. Opinions vary as to the
      reliability of these documents.

14   See *A Celtic Pilgrimage*, p.39, for discussion of Celtic saints in
      Somerset.

15   See *A Pilgrimage around Wales*, p.123.

16   For details of the Romanesque lead fonts in Gloucestershire (all
      the others are still in situ, with one being in the parish church in
      nearby Tidenham), see the website of Urban Archaeology.

17   One of the features of the woodland at Lancaut, and in the lower
      Wye Valley in general, is the large number of yew trees (*taxus
      baccata*). Unlike the many very venerable specimens to be found
      in Welsh churchyards, these 'wild' trees do not appear to survive
      to a great age.

18   ... *our barge drawing too much water to pass the shallows, till the
      return of the tide...* Gilpin, p.59.

19   An excellent guide to the area, intended for canoeists, includes
      mention of Lancaut on p. 27. Layout 1 (wyevalleyaonb.org.uk)

20   For some of Turner's preliminary work at Ewenny, see the Tate
      Modern gallery's website.

21   To view the painting online, see the Collections Online section of
      the website of National Museum Wales.

22   For details of the screen, see the website of the architects Caroe
      and Partners. Alexander Beleschenko also designed the glass
      roundel in the centre of the *Siambr* in the Senedd Cymru (Welsh
      Parliament).

23   For further photos and an explanation of the arrangement
      between Cadw and the Church in Wales as regards the site, see
      the Monastic Wales website.

24   An aerial view of Dylife, showing the outline of the foundations
      of St David's Church and also the graveyard can be found on the
      Coflein website.

25   The pub's car park is a venue for stargazing in its dark sky
      location in the Cambrian Mountains.

26   Further local information and photos can be seen on the website
      www.abandonedcommunities.co.uk

27   The evidence for Roman extraction and processing of lead at
      Dylife is taken from an account of a visit to the mines in the
      1850s by David Davies of the Cambrian Archaeological Society.
      He was shown what was claimed to be the remains of a Roman
      lead-smelting furnace.

28   The name of one of the slate quarries at Blaenau Ffestiniog, the
     Fotty, was taken from that of an adjacent farm with the name of
     Haffotty, this being derived from *hafotai*.
29   For a detailed discussion of how pre-industrial tracks have
     shaped the landscape and development of the town, see 'Blaenau
     Ffestiniog: Understanding Urban Character on the Welsh Slate'
     (Llechi Cymru website).
30   In the census of 1921, a useful list of different occupations
     within slate mining was compiled to assist those who went door-
     to-door to complete accurate returns.

Chapter 10: Go ye into all the world

1   Gospel of St Mark, 15:16, KJV.
2   See *A Pilgrimage around Wales*, p. 101.
3   Originally founded as the British and Foreign Bible Society,
    retelling of the story can be found on the Bible Society's website.
4   One of the Bibles acquired by Mary Jones is in the Bible Society
    archive at Cambridge University, with another Bible in the
    collection of the National Library of Wales believed to be one of
    the other copies. The whereabouts of the third is unknown.
5   Mary is thought to have walked barefoot but today's walkers,
    with boots and waterproofs, can follow the instructions for the
    Mary Jones Walk (*Taith Mary Jones*) which are on information
    boards along the route.
6   The 1919 edition of the book is also available in digital format on
    the Internet Archive website.
7   For details of the Caer Gai Roman fort see the website of the
    Gwynedd Archaeological Trust (*Ymddiriedolaeth Archaeolegol
    Gwynedd*). It is also of interest that an early Christian incised
    stone with a Latin inscription was found at the site in the
    seventeenth century, although its whereabouts are now
    unknown.
8   The mill dates back to at least the seventeenth century and is a
    Grade II listed building.
9   It has been maintained that Alexander Burgh Lish (1814–1852)
    had earlier laid the foundation for this.
10 The lives of both Thomas Jones and Robert Jermain Thomas
    belong firmly in the era of the chartered trading companies.
    These bodies were rapidly opening up mercantile links, in
    effect as agents of the rapidly-prospering nations of Western
    Europe. In the case of the British East India Company, the
    enclaves and wealth it was able to secure what would lead to the
    establishment of British rule in India.
11 It should be noted that there is some opposition to the

predominance of Christianity in Khasi society. See the article 'The Traditional Religion of the Khasis' (January 2016) on the website of the *Shillong Times*.

12   The Presbyterian Church of India takes the arrival of Thomas Jones 'the First Missionary' as the date of its foundation. The Khasi Hills also experienced a Revival among the Christian community in 1905–06, following on from the 1904–05 Revival in Wales.

13   See the website of Welsh and Khasi Cultural Dialogues.

14   See the article 'Why Celebrate Thomas Jones Day' in the *Shillong Times* (June 2018).

15   Hanover Chapel is also well-known amongst the Korean community in Britain. When I arrived at the seaside town of Morecambe in Lancashire on my way to the Isle of Man, I was intrigued to meet a local hotelier of Korean descent who knew all about the chapel and Robert Jermain Thomas.

16   Llandovery College was founded by Thomas Phillips in 1847 to provide a liberal and Classical education alongside the study of Welsh language, history and literature.

17   New College, London, was formed from three pre-existing dissenting academies for the purposes of educating congregationalist ministers. It eventually became part of the University of London, but now exists as the charity New College London Foundation, with the object of supporting 'the training for men and women for the Christian ministry, particularly for the ministry in the United Reformed Church'.

18   Founded in 1809, this is now the Scottish Bible Society.

19   For a comprehensive study of the history of Korea from a Roman Catholic and Jesuit perspective, see the very informative 'The Society of Jesus and Korea: A Historiographical Essay' by Jieun Han and Franklin Rausch. This is available on the website of Brill Academic Publishers.

20   For some useful comments on the Confucian cultural background in Korea, see pp. 5–6 in *Protestant Pioneers in Korea* by Everett Nichols Hunt, Jr. (New York, 1980). This is available on the Internet Archive website.

21   I am very grateful to Stella Price for her research into the details of Thomas' journeys to Korea and, in particular, the circumstances surrounding his death. Her observation that earlier Jesuit activity in Korea would not have included the distribution of Bibles is especially apt.

22   The organisation Open Doors has consistently placed North Korea (officially known as the Democratic People's Republic of Korea) at the top of its country rankings as regards the severity of persecution faced by Christians.

23   215 Like Robert Jermain Thomas, Gütlaff was a very gifted
      linguist. For a brief biography and catalogue of his many
      writings (in various languages) and works of translation, see
      Alexander Wylie's *Protestant Missions to the Chinese* which was
      published in 1867. This is available on the Internet Archive
      website as is Gütlaff's own *Journal of three voyages along the
      coast of China... with notices of Siam, Corea and the Loo-Choo
      Islands*.

Chapter 11: The twentieth century and the new millennium

1   The Disestablishment Bill was introduced in the House of
      Commons in 1912 and received the Royal Assent in September
      1914. However, the outbreak of the Great War resulted in delay
      in implementing the legislation.

2   For discussion of similar issues as regards the creation of
      the reservoir at Lake Vyrnwy (*Llyn Efyrnwy*) in mid Wales,
      completed in 1888 and also built for the Corporation of
      Liverpool, see *A Pilgrimage around Wales*, p. 143.

3   For a painting of the Tryweryn valley, probably completed
      in 1911, by James Dickson Innes, see the website
      abandonedcommunities.co.uk

4   For details of the campaign mounted by the Capel Celyn Defence
      Committee, see the website abandonedcommunities.co.uk

5   Gwynfor Evans went on to be Plaid Cymru's first MP at
      Westminster, being elected to represent Carmarthenshire in
      1966.

6   See a report, 'Tryweryn: Personal stories 50 years after
      drowning', which is available on the BBC News website.

7   See the Visits page on the website of Our Lady of Fatima Bala.

8   By tradition, the town of Fatima gets its Arabic-derived name
      from that of a Moorish princess abducted during Muslim rule on
      the Iberian peninsula in the later Middle Ages.

9   The Loreto Sisters are a religious order founded by a Catholic
      Englishwoman, Mary Ward, in France in 1609.

10   For more details, and a photo, of the artwork the *Miracle of the
      Spinning Sun* see the website of Stained Glass in Wales (*Gwydr
      Lliw yng Nghymru*).

11   For more details of the route and an interactive map see the Via
      Beata website.

12   Gospel of St John 6: 68. The inscription in English uses the New
      King James Version, whereas the inscription in Welsh uses the
      Beibl Cymraeg Newydd Diwygiedig, 2004.

Chapter 12: The early saints revisited

1 The Welsh place-name component *Merthyr* is derived from the
Latin *martyrium*, meaning a shrine associated with the death
of a martyr (correctly, a witness) or their relics. As such, it may
be an indication of a very early ecclesiastical site. For further
discussion, see *A Pilgrimage Around Wales*, p. 124.

2 The earliest text of the *The Life of Samson of Dol* that is available
to us today dates from the early eleventh century. It was
translated by Thomas Taylor and published in English in 1925.

3 What little we know of Tydfil is included in *An Essay on the
Welsh Saints* by the Rev. Rice Rees (1804–1839), published in
1836. This is available on the Internet Archive website.

4 Herrad, p. 142.

5 Ibid., p. 141.

6 The footpaths make a circular walk within the Cwm Taf Fechan
Nature Reserve. For more details see the Croeso Merthyr
website.

7 Herrad, p. 149.

8 Another parish church, dedicated to St David, in a more central
position in the town was opened in 1847.

9 In the Royal Commission on the Ancient and Historical
Monuments of Wales' inventory of the ancient monuments of
Glamorgan of 1976, the cross was described as a 'simply incised
ringed cross [which] has expanded terminals of trifid form and
on the stem'.

10 Taylor, p. 8.

11 Ibid.

12 Ibid., p. 14.

13 Ibid., p. 34.

14 Ibid., p. 39.

15 It should be noted that Dyfed had seen settlement from Ireland
from the later Roman period until about 500 and that the
area of Caldey probably experienced considerable sea-borne
traffic to and from Ireland including, as here, those who were
passing through to and from the continent of Europe. It may
also have been the case that Samson's family had connections
with Ireland. In addition, a stone dating from the fifth to sixth
century, inscribed with Ogham (as well as Latin) can be seen in
St David's Church on the island, providing further evidence of
the close connections between this area of west Wales, including
Caldey, and Ireland. For information on Ogham, particularly in
relation to south and west Wales, see the Visiting section on the
website of Pilgrim Street Contemporary Pilgrimage.

16 Both the Cornish churches use the spelling 'Sampson' in their
dedication, with both spellings being used more generally with

reference to the saint in English. However, in French, it is always 'Samson'.

17   For more details of the South Hill inscribed stone, see the website of Historic England.

18   Taylor, p. 49.

19   *Archaeology Report 2002* in the possession of the churchwardens and PCC of St Sampson's Church, South Hill. A possible missing component in South Hill's claim to be the site of Samson's monastery in Cornwall seems to be the lack of a cave in the vicinity, as mentioned in the *Life* on page 51.

20   Recognised as a cathedral and bishopric by the ninth century, the later building on the site then lost this status in the early nineteenth century following the French Revolution. Since 1880 the cathedral and its diocese have been part of the Archbishopric of Rennes, Dol and St Malo (*Arc'heskopti Roazhon Dol ha Sant-Maloù*).

21   Guernsey is thought to be the *Lesia* of the Latin text. Taylor, p. 75. Also see the Guernsey Donkey website for Samson's life from a Channel Islands perspective.

22   The resulting report is available online. See Anglo-Saxon, Norse & Celtic: St Samson Colloquy Report (anglosaxonnorseandceltic. blogspot.com).

23   Taylor, p. 5.

24   A very useful summary of more recent scholarship can be found on the Cambridge Core website in a review by Ali Bonner of *St Samson of Dol and the Earliest History of Brittany, Cornwall and Wales*, edited by Lynette Olson.

25   For details of the project as a whole and an accompanying map, see the website of the City Centre Mural Trail Glasgow.

26   Smug is also known as Smug One and Sam Bates.

27   Jocelin's *Life of Kentigern* (Mungo) is available translated into English by Cynthia Whiddon Green, together with very useful notes. The story of 'the redbird (so called) by the common people because of its ruby-colored small body' is found in chapter 5. Cynthia Whiddon Green's translation accompanies her thesis, *Saint Kentigern, Apostle to Strathclyde: A critical analysis of a northern saint* which includes helpful discussion of the relationship between the northern British kingdoms in the sixth century and Wales and Ireland. Both Cynthia Whiddon Green's translation and her thesis are available on the website of Fordham University.

28   Cadwallon Llawhir *(Long hand)*, thought to have been king of Gwynedd in the first two decades of the sixth century.

29   See note 249 in Cynthia Whiddon Green's translation for a very interesting discussion of this charter. This note also deals with

the issue of church dedications on Anglesey to saints thought to
be associated with Mungo.

30   For details of Rederech, see chapter 29 of Jocelin's Life of
      Kentigern and note 240 by Cynthia Whiddon Green.

31   The other two churches dedicated to Tydecho are at Cemmaes
      (*Cemaes*) and at Garthbeibio, both just inside Powys. Tydecho's
      association with a fifth site on a hillside above the village of
      Aberangell, just south of Mallwyd, is very uncertain. There is
      also a medieval chapel site associated with Tydecho in Llanberis
      on Anglesey.

32   *Cywydd* is a traditional form of Welsh poetry which follows a
      strict metrical pattern.

33   This is believed to refer to Maelgwyn Gwynedd (also known by
      the Latinised form of his name, Maglocunus) who was king of
      Gwynedd and died in about 547. Maelgwyn is thought to have
      been a descendant of Cunedda.

34   Edwards' translation of the two poems into English is available
      online. See 'The Works of the Rev. Griffith Edwards' which can
      be found on the Google Books website.

35   In *A Guide to Dinas Mawddwy* (Aberystwyth, 1893), the historian
      Charles Ashton (1848–1899) also mentions *Buches Dydecho*
      (Tydecho's cowfold), close to the Llaethnant. He comments that
      the incident whereby the saint turned the water of the stream
      into milk was prompted by his maid accidentally spilling her
      buckets of fresh milk, a story that is not included in the late
      medieval sources. Ashton's guide (Dinas Mawddwy is a village
      between Mallwyd and Llanymawddwy) is available online on
      Google Books.

36   For more information about the yew tree at Llanymawddwy,
      see the website of the Ancient Yew group. Also, for yew trees
      in Welsh churchyards more generally, see *A Pilgrimage around
      Wales*, pp. 108–110.

37   A photograph of the font (sadly surrounded by detritus) can be
      seen online on Paul Challinor's website, Travels with my Aunt.
      At the time of writing, the future of the church was the subject of
      consultation in the local area.

38   It is possible to continue the walk as a long, circular route,
      making one's way along the public footpath up to the fence
      line at Bwlch Sirddyn and then up onto Esgeiriau Gwynion
      and thence to the viewpoint on the road near Bwlch y Groes.
      However, boggy terrain and extensive peat hags make this a very
      challenging walk, although a guide is available on the Outdoors
      GPS website.

39   See the website of the Ancient Yew Group.

Select Bibliography

Aldhouse-Green, Miranda and Howell, Ray, *Celtic Wales* (University of Wales Press, 2000).

Bowen, E.G., *The Settlements of the Celtic Saints in Wales* (Cardiff, 1954).

Coplestone-Crow, Bruce, *Herefordshire Place-names* (Logaston Press, 2009)

Davies, John, *A History of Wales* (Penguin Books, 1994).

Davies, Norman, *Europe A History* (Pimlico, 1997).

Davies, W., *Wales in the early Middle Ages* (Leicester, 1982).

Evans, E., *Early Mediaeval Ecclesiastical Sites in South-East Wales* (Cadw, 2003).

Fletcher, Richard, *The Conversion of Europe* (Harper Collins, 1997).

Gregory, D., *Country Churchyards of Wales* (Llanrwst, 2002).

Herrad, Imogen Ria, *The Woman who Loved an Octopus and Other Saints' Tales* (Seren, 2007).

Hill, Christopher, *The World Turned Upside Down* (Maurice Temple Smith, 1972).

Hughes, T.J., *Wales' Best One Hundred Churches* (Seren, 2007).

Humphries, Peter, *On the Trail of Turner* (Cadw, 1995).

Manning, William, *Roman Wales* (Cardiff, 2001).

Morgans, John I., *The Honest Heretique* (Y Lolfa, 2012).

Morgans, John I. and Noble, Peter C., *Our Holy Ground* (Y Lolfa, 2016).

Morris, Philip, *Llanilltud: The story of a Celtic Christian Community* (Y Lolfa, 2020).

Neill, Stephen, *A History of Christian Missions* (Penguin Books, 1964).

Petts, David, *The Early Medieval Church in Wales* (Stroud, 2009).

Price, Stella, *Chosen for Choson (Korea): Robert Jermain Thomas* (Emmaus Road Ministries, 2003).

Rees, Elizabeth, *Celtic Saints of Wales* (Fonthill Media, 2015).

Siberry, Elizabeth and Wilcher, Robert (eds), *Henry Vaughan and the Usk Valley* (Logaston Press, 2016).

Taylor, Thomas, *The Life of St Samson of Dol* (SPCK, 1925).

Thurlby, Malcolm, *Romanesque Architecture and Sculpture in Wales* (Logaston Press, 2006).

Thurlby, Malcolm, *The Herefordshire School of Romanesque Sculpture* (Logaston Press, 2013).

Williams, Michael Aufrere, 'Medieval English Roodscreens, with special reference to Devon' (Ph.D. thesis, 2008).

Index

Also by the author:

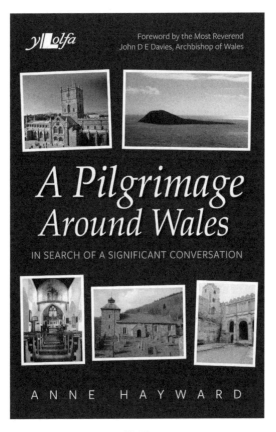

£8.99

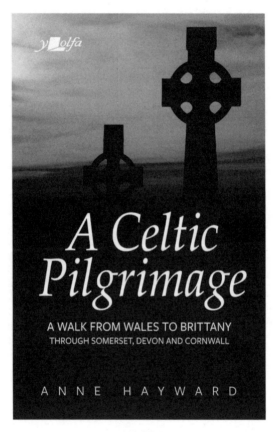

A Celtic
Pilgrimage

A WALK FROM WALES TO BRITTANY
THROUGH SOMERSET, DEVON AND CORNWALL

ANNE HAYWARD

£8.99

Also from Y Lolfa:

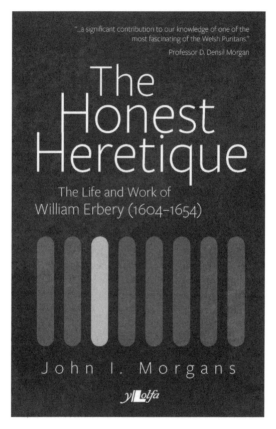

"...a significant contribution to our knowledge of one of the
most fascinating of the Welsh Puritans."
Professor D. Densil Morgan

The
Honest
Heretique

The Life and Work of
William Erbery (1604–1654)

John I. Morgans

y Lolfa

£14.95

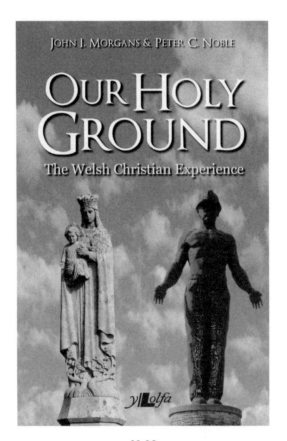

JOHN I. MORGANS & PETER C. NOBLE

OUR HOLY GROUND

The Welsh Christian Experience

y Lolfa

£9.99

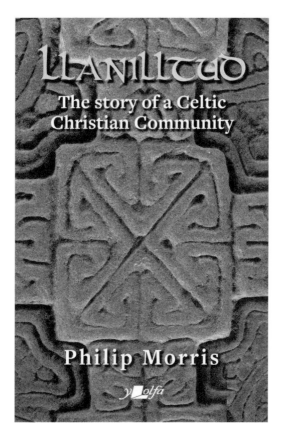

LLANILLTUD

The story of a Celtic
Christian Community

Philip Morris

y Lolfa

£9.99